GUIDE TO THE
DOGS
OF THE WORLD

GUIDE TO THE
DOGS
OF THE WORLD

A. Gondrexon-Ives Browne

Illustrated by K. van den Broecke

Consultant Editor H. Glover

TREASURE PRESS

First published in Great Britain by The Hamlyn Publishing Group Ltd
Planned and produced by Elsevier Publishing Projects S.A., Lausanne

This edition published by Treasure Press
59 Grosvenor Street
London W1

Reprinted 1984

© 1974 Elsevier Publishing Projects S.A., Lausanne
ISBN 0 907812 17 1

Printed in Czechoslovakia
50492/2

Contents

Foreword

As the interest in pedigree dogs is increasing all over the world, it seemed useful to bring together in a handy and not too expensive volume the well-known, the less known and the unknown breeds that, generally speaking, are only found in large encyclopaedias of dogs.

It has been the author's aim to meet the demands of two kinds of reader. Firstly, those readers who are interested in the cynological matter and wish to gain more knowledge of the great many extant breeds. This book will show them to which breed a dog belongs, its origins and for what purpose it is or was used. Secondly, those readers who require help in their choice of a purebred dog and useful information on keeping a dog.

Since about three hundred breeds had to be described and illustrated, the descriptions had to be very succinct and only those particulars from the standards have been mentioned which, together with the pictures, help to give a clear idea of the different breeds. The data was obtained from the original standards of the breeds' countries of origin as recognized by the Fédération Cynologique Internationale (FCI). An exception to this rule has been made whenever distinct differences occur between these standards and the English or American ones.

Purebred, though not recognized working breeds, such as the Foxhound, the Otterhound, etc. have been included. For nearly all breeds the height at withers is mentioned, but in a few cases this was not possible as the standards only mention weights. As far as possible the original names of breeds—that is, those used in the countries of origin—are mentioned.

The author, who has received much love from her many dog companions all her life, hopes to have contributed with this guide to the spread of some general cynological knowledge. She hopes that it will be of use in the choice, the rearing and the care of a dog and she wishes her readers a lot of enriching experience in the world of dogs.

A.G.-I.B.

Introduction

The choice of a dog

There are many reasons why people decide to keep a dog and find themselves faced with the question: 'which kind of dog shall I choose?' They may be looking for a replacement for a lost, faithful and trusted housemate; they may need a companion because they live alone; they may want a playmate for their children and a way of teaching them responsibility and care for other creatures; they may seek a pet to share the life of a childless home; or they may wish to acquire a status symbol to compete with the lady next door who attracts so much attention with her strikingly fashionable dog. Whatever the reason for wanting a pet no-one should rashly rush into acquiring a dog. They should not only consider their own interests as prospective owners but, first and foremost, think of the happiness of their future companion.

If you choose your dog with care your life will be enriched for years by a friend who will give much love and satisfaction and cause little annoyance. If, on the other hand, a dog is acquired without forethought or only because of its looks you will risk being bitterly disappointed.

A dog placed in unsuitable, uncongenial surroundings will feel unhappy and will not show his true character. It may become sullen and start growling and misbehaving, perhaps even becoming so undisciplined and aggressive that it proves unacceptable to his new owner, who will blame the failure on the animal or its breed instead of admitting that the fault lay in his ill-considered choice. In keeping a pet the owner is taking on a considerable responsibility, and if, for instance, the pet is only wanted as a status symbol it would be best to think again.

The first question to ask yourself is whether your way of life and personal circumstances allow you to keep a dog. The time which you can make available for the dog is very important. It is necessary to be able to give it sufficient attention, because no dog can do without it. You need time to prepare his meals, to give it its daily brush, to take it for a walk for at least an hour a day and moreover to let it out two or three times a day, which means going with him and not letting him loose alone on the street.

A second, no less important question concerns the attitudes of all the members of the family. Is everybody happy with the idea of having a dog? Its arrival may give rise to friction. Children so easily promise to look after and take out their new companion, but as soon as the novelty wears off they forget the responsibilities they have undertaken. It is vital that the mistress of the house wants to have a dog, for it is she who, during the absence of her husband and children, will probably have most to do with the new housepet. She may have to cope with the less agreeable jobs such as cleaning up the mud which will be brought into the house in bad weather, removing dog hairs from carpets and furniture and coping with those other little mishaps which occur. On her will fall the main burden of house-training the dog if it is a young one, and looking after it if it is ill.

If all the family are agreed that they want a dog there is another problem to consider. What is to be done with the dog during holidays? Can it always be taken along? If not, are there friends able and ready to offer it hospitality, or will it have to go to a boarding kennel? In the latter case you should not wait until the day before leaving to look around for a good—a really good—kennel. As you might expect boarding out your dog may prove quite expensive; expenses that must be added to the dog licences (which are quite high in some countries and towns), the unavoidable vet's bills and the cost of food—you should not economize on the quality. Remember that any possession that brings joy also involves care and responsibility and a dog is no exception. If, after considering all these points, you still have an unquenchable desire to own a dog your next problem will be to decide what kind of dog to choose.

A pedigree dog or not?

A dog is no less an individual than a human being, and any dog, purebred or not, will have its own personality. A mongrel can be just as faithful and affectionate as a pedigree, and may be equally playful or lazy, aggressive or friendly, bold or shy. The pedigree dog, however, has the great advantage that its appearance can be forecast and its character more or less predicted while it is still a puppy. Individual features will manifest themselves in each animal but all members of a breed will tend to have the same natural disposition. A dog belonging to a sheep-herding breed, for instance, will be a good watchdog and ready to defend his own; a terrier is enterprising and gay; a hound is self-willed and possesses a strong hunting instinct. The purebred dog will remain true to type, which makes it easier to choose a puppy which will grow up to suit your taste, requirements, and circumstances.

A quite different consideration which may lead you to prefer a pedigree is that if you should breed from your pet a more attractive result could be expected than would be the case with a mongrel. A promising litter can be bred out of a beautiful, sound, and

A delightful little puppy may develop into a huge dog crowding you out of the room.

purebred bitch and a well-chosen sire. You should be warned, however, that such a litter will demand a great deal of caring for and involve considerable expense which will scarcely be made up by the sale of puppies—you should have no illusions about that! Nevertheless, it is an enjoyable experience to see a litter of puppies grow up from day to day.

If you have no strong desire for a dog of a definite breed you will probably find a wide choice among those unfortunate dogs waiting for a kind master and a good home in local kennels for strays. Most of them will be mongrels, that is dogs whose parents do not belong to the same breed. Sometimes they are crosses of two purebred dogs of different breeds, but usually are a mixture of many breeds because one of the parents, or both, was already a mongrel. Of course, a mongrel can be as agreeable a companion as a pedigree dog, and it may be a very handsome animal even though its appearance does not conform to the standard for a pedigree breed. If it is a very young dog its future appearance and its character are both unpredictable. Fortunately, there are always people who are prepared to leave this to chance. The risk involved is naturally less with a fully-grown dog, because then you are seeing a dog with character and appearance that have matured and you can decide with more certainty whether it matches your own wishes. Do not forget, however that a foundling who has perhaps been badly treated and then kept in a dog's home for days, will not show its most attractive side; a shy, surly stray may develop into an ideal companion in new, loving surroundings.

You would certainly be doing a worthwhile thing by adopting a stray, but it is an action that requires much thought. There may be a reason why a dog has landed in the dog pound, and if this reason lies in its bad qualities, they may not become apparent until you have owned the dog for some time. In such a case you must be willing to devote yourself entirely to facing the problems that arise. It is inhumane to release an animal from its misery only to cast it out later. The well-meant, but ill-considered deed could end in a tragedy. The acquisition of a mongrel incurs the same degree of responsibility as the purchase of an expensive pedigree dog.

There is a widespread misconception that a mongrel will be stronger and more resistant to disease than a purebred dog. Those who have worked in a dog's home know better.

If, notwithstanding all the arguments that plead for the rescue of a creature in need, you decide in favour of a purebred dog, you should first consider which natural qualities you want in the dog.

Once you have determined the group to which the dog should belong—sheep-herding, terrier, mastiff, hound, gundog, or companion dog—there usually still remains a great diversity in size and coat. You should carefully consider the conditions in which the new dog will have to live. No large, long-coated breed fits easily into a flat; no sporting dog should be deprived of all opportunity to run as its heart desires; nor is a hound suited to a neighbourhood of open fields or woods where, following its hunting instinct, it may get lost. Do not forget that the grooming of a rough- or long-coated dog demands much more time than that of a smooth-haired breed, and that the trimming required by the former may be rather expensive. If you object to this, you will soon possess a dog which looks quite different from those of the type chosen. A similar thing may happen if, without knowledge of the breed, you cannot resist the appeal of a delightful little puppy which after six months or so develops into a huge dog crowding you out of the room.

To help you decide on the breed, if your choice is not yet fixed, you can visit dog shows. The amateur would do well to study the many illustrations and descriptions of the various breeds which make up this book.

As soon as you have narrowed down your choice you can get more detailed information from the specialized clubs which exist for most breeds. These clubs have been founded by owners and breeders with the object of looking after the interests of a special breed or group of breeds, and they are willing to give any information required. The addresses of the secretaries of these clubs can be obtained from the kennel club of every country.

If you want impartial expert advice you should do as suggested above. Be wary of buying a dog through one of the many advertisements in the newspapers, because these dogs can come from dealers or back-yard breeders who are only out for gain. These people mate two dogs of the same breed without considering whether it is an acceptable combination or not; they breed much too often with the same bitch and they give the dam and the puppies poor and insufficient food. Therefore, there is a great risk that something may go wrong with the puppy and then, apart from the disappointment, the trouble and the vet's bills, nothing can be done about it. This is also the case when, as may occur, the seller promises to send the pedigree of the young dog and fails to do so. At the same time these dealers ask a price for their puppies equal to that for a young animal bred with care and expert knowledge by a *bona fide* breeder out of love of the breed.

Dog or bitch?

Once you have decided on the type of dog you want, the question is whether you prefer a dog or a bitch. This may depend on individual considerations, but just as is the case with the choice of a breed, the circumstances and the environment where the dog will live and the 'use' you wish to make of it must be considered. The chosen breed may also be of influence on the choice of sex. If you cannot decide, the best thing to do is to ask those who are experienced in the breed and contact the breed clubs or the kennel club.

Generally a dog has a stronger personality than a bitch, which makes him more difficult to train. A firmer handling is needed to let him know, from the beginning, who is the master, and to teach him obedience. He is more pugnacious than the bitch, which with some breeds may create difficulties. It is easier for the owner of a well-kept garden to train a bitch not to soil the beautiful lawn than to make a dog understand that he should not urinate against shrubs and plants. As a matter of fact, the male likes to put his scent everywhere, and with him this is more likely to happen indoors too. If many bitches happen to live in the neighbourhood, the dog may be very difficult and restless at times, refuse all food and lose condition. There is also the danger that he will take advantage of a door carelessly left ajar and run to the bitch's home and remain there on the doorstep for days. Perhaps this is the reason why the dog is sometimes presumed to be less faithful than the bitch, quite unjustly because it is just a matter of natural instinct. For the same reason a bitch cannot always be taken out. Twice a year she will be on heat and in order to avoid an unwanted litter she must be kept on a tight lead or shut up safely. If unwanted mating does happen the vet will be able to prevent whelping by an injection, provided this is done within one or two days of the mating. However, the bitch will then come on heat again, so prevention is far better than cure. It is very difficult to find homes for a litter of mongrels, especially if you try to find good homes and are reluctant to take away all the puppies from the dam immediately after the birth. The bitch can be given a hormone injection to prevent her coming on heat, but this certainly should not be recommended; in my view it cannot be sound to interfere again and again with a natural function. Moreover, after one or more injections, the season often stays away altogether for some time so that you are prevented from breeding if you should want to do so. This does not matter so much with older bitches—a bitch comes into season till a very old age—because you should not breed from them. Apart from all this, much trouble can be avoided by giving the bitch on heat chlorophyll tablets especially made for this purpose.

If you seriously consider breeding a litter, have enough time and are prepared to take all the trouble involved, it should give you great pleasure. If a reasonably sized litter of good quality is produced their sale may just about cover the cost of the care and feeding of the dam, the vet's assistance if necessary, the various injections needed and the rearing of the newborn puppies, but it will not produce a profit. If you own a beautiful dog you will have to wait until someone wants to use him to mate with their bitch. Without the trouble, or the joy, of rearing a litter the owner of the sire usually has the right of having the pick of the litter or a fee equal to the price of one puppy.

The puppy

Choice and first care
It is difficult to pick out the most promising puppy from a litter aged six or seven weeks. Unless you are already an expert you should certainly ask for the advice of someone with a knowledge of the breed in question and of puppies. Even if you do not particularly want a dog of show-quality, it will still be necessary to give full attention to the behaviour of the puppies. A bold little dog will be better able to maintain itself later on in a noisy family than will be the case with a timid or shy dog. All the puppies should show a bold disposition and both they and the dam have a well-fed look.

Opinions differ as to what age the puppy should be when it is acquired. The American Dr Scott has made psychological tests with puppies of very varying type and has found that seven to eight weeks is the age at which the best adaption to the new master and the new surroundings may be expected. Among wild animals the male usually starts the education of the young, a task which in the case of pets must be taken over by the master. Many breeders do not let the puppies go before they are three months old, because they can then have been given all the vaccinations required. If the puppy is collected by the new owner at eight weeks, the breeder should have already given him a worm cure twice and the puppy should have had the distemper and hard pad vaccinations. This provisional vaccination can be given from the fifth week onwards. The vet then gives a certificate of vaccination which specifies the date when the definite vaccination, which should also protect against hepatitis (liver disease) and lepto-spirose (disease of Weil), should be given. Some vaccinations must be repeated but the vet will give all the necessary information. Also ask him when and how you must give the puppy a worm cure again, and do not forget to keep its nails short.

The change to new surroundings will certainly be easier if the puppy is not older than two months. Its resistance will then be less, and after a tiring day full of new impressions, it will, when left alone, fall asleep with little protest. The older puppy, which has become more strongly tied to his original surroundings, will be much more upset by the change. It will object by howling and its greater strength will enable it to prolong its protest. The events of the first night are often decisive for the future, so it is wise to fetch the dog during the morning to give it an opportunity to settle down.

As a first sleeping place a medium-sized wooden box with a

A bold little dog will be better able to maintain itself later on in a noisy family than a timid or shy dog.

layer of newspapers on the bottom is highly recommended. It is advisable to provide a well-wrapped stone or metal hot-water bottle, which will replace the warmth of the litter companions. It is a good idea to construct a small run—a baby's pen with the sides covered with fine netting is appropriate—and cover the floor with a thick layer of folded newspapers. The puppy, not yet able to control its needs during the whole night, will relieve itself in this run, which will avoid soiling the house and enable any mess to be rapidly cleaned up.

The best way to house-train a dog during the daytime is to let it out immediately after its meals and its naps and also every one and a half or two hours. A dog is an animal of habit, and by preventing it from doing something in the house it becomes accustomed to doing it outside. During bad weather the puppy can be led to some newspapers in the shower, on a covered

A baby's pen used as a run is the best place to leave the young dog when you have to go out.

16

balcony or somewhere where things will not be soiled and when it has finished, reward it with some cheese, apple or meat. Newspaper training is also practical for people living in a flat. It will, however, be a little difficult later on to teach the dog to relieve itself out of doors. Just as is the case with children, some puppies are able to be clean much sooner than others.

A dog basket within the run is the best place to leave the young dog when you have to go out or when it is impossible constantly to keep an eye on it. It will prevent accidents and the destruction of your belongings. See to it that it has something to play with—a ball or a toy bone made of ox-hide are ideal and can be bought in every pet shop. Never give him anything made of rubber, because any small pieces it may gnaw off and swallow could block it's intestines, whereas the ox-hide may be eaten without any danger. Old shoes or slippers, with their nails and dye, are also a source of risk.

Feeding

At first you must keep to the diet that the puppy is used to, even though it may not have been the ideal food. If the food is altered at the same time as the change in environment, the danger of tummy-upsets, leading to diarrhoea, is increased. Always ask what food the dog has been accustomed to; a good breeder will provide a feeding chart. If you want to alter the composition of the meals you must introduce changes very gradually and never before the puppy feels absolutely at home.

Naturally, there are many ways of making an eight-week old puppy grow into a strong, healthy dog. After a year, the representatives of most breeds will still be maturing, but they will not grow any taller. At that age, the greatest danger of deformities resulting from a deficient diet is past. Between two and three months a puppy must be given five meals a day; between three and five months, four meals; and between five and nine months, three meals. When he is older than nine months he must be fed twice a day. Most young dogs are fond of cereals with milk, but at four months this should be replaced by stale brown bread. Proteins should be the principal ingredient of the daily food and they can be given as horsemeat, beef, bullock's heart, tripe or fish (if tripe, give almost a double portion). Everything should be cut up very finely. Depending on the size of the breed, the food is cut up less finely as the puppy grows older. Heart and fish must be cooked, all the other meats can be given raw. Thoroughly remove the skin and bones from the fish. Eggs and milk are also excellent for the growing dog; the eggs should be soft-boiled, and some cream or a lump of butter or margarine added to the milk, as the bitch's milk is heavier than cow's milk. Very finely-shredded and lightly-boiled greens and tomatoes or orange juice will provide some vitamins.

It goes without saying that quantities and requirements differ from breed to breed; you can get information from the breeder (provided he is an expert), the breed club or the vet. They too can tell you everything about the right amounts of vitamins, calcium and minerals which must be present in the daily ration. Fresh water should always be available, but do not let the dog drink just before or after its meal.

Bringing up your dog
Let the puppy have a fixed place in the house, where it can lie down comfortably, as this will prevent it from using chairs. The

Every dog should have its own bed in a warm, quiet, draught-free place.

dog must be taught from youth what is and what is not allowed. Do not waver in your discipline and be consistent in your rules, to reprove the dog for something one day and permit it the next will only make the dog confused. If you allow the puppy things which will be forbidden to the adult dog, this will lead to difficulties later on because it is not easy to break a habit. The little animal must be treated with great patience. Always use the same words to teach it something, for instance, 'good dog' when all goes well and 'no' or 'shame' in the opposite case. Never punish or beat it, even if it has been unclean, because this will just scare it and make it insecure. If it relieves itself in the room this proves that it has not yet understood that this should be done only out of doors or in a special place. It is best to pick the puppy up immediately and put it down outside. If the mishap is discovered

Examples of well-constructed dog houses.

too late, then you should ignore it. It is senseless to punish a dog, be it young or old, for a deed it does not recollect. Take it for a walk in the morning and in the afternoon, because this will give it an opportunity to use up its energy.

The adult dog

Feeding

An adult dog should preferably be given two meals a day. One daily meal may be adequate for an overweight or old dog, but it is better for a young, active animal not to get all its food at once. Moreover, the meal is generally a feast for a healthy dog, so why not give the dog this pleasure twice a day? It is best to give a light meal in the morning and the principal meal in the afternoon. Never feed the dog just before daily exercise.

As a rule, the adult dog will thrive on the same food as was recommended for the puppy but the proportions will be different. In this case too the requirements will vary from breed to breed, and it is advisable to ask a good breeder or the breed club for directions about the right way of feeding. In any case, never spare animal proteins. A dog, descendant of a wolf, was originally a carnivore, and although in the course of time it has become an omnivore, flesh, offal or fish must remain the main constituents of the diet, supplemented with milk, cheese, eggs, bread, vegetables and fruit. You will do well to give about one ounce of heart, horsemeat or fish for every two pounds of the animal's own weight, but when

The feeder of a large dog should be placed on a wooden bench or stool.

feeding offal, give half as much again. Fresh drinking water should always be available. If the dog comes home thirsty just before his mealtime, let it drink first and postpone the meal for an hour or so.

Nowadays there are many ready-made compound foods for the dog containing everything it needs in the right proportions. If you choose a really good one among the many brands for sale, this will do very well as a first meal or to take on a trip if need be. Some lazy people serve only dry or canned food to their pet day in day out. In this way the dog may get enough food, but it takes away the pleasure of eating. A dog no more appreciates getting the same food every day than a human being, it just is not able to say so. In some countries, not alas in Britain, manufacturers are bound by law to state the content of their pet foods. If you serve proprietary dog food to your dog find out what it contains so that you can balance the diet.

Care and grooming

Nearly all breeds need regular brushing, if only to control the nuisance of dog hairs in the house. Both the brushes and the way of brushing will differ according to the various coats. Keep the dog free from fleas, because they are carriers of worm's eggs and the itch they cause will make the dog scratch and bite itself causing eczema. Fleas attack dogs during the warm summer months especially, but good deterrents are available at any pet shop. To avoid splay-feet the nails should be kept short. With dogs that always exercise on a hard surface, the nails will wear down naturally; if not, they should be trimmed with clippers or filed at regular times. Let the vet or the pet shop show you how to do this the first time. The teeth can be kept free of tartar with hydrogen peroxide. To control infection the ears must be regularly cleaned using a little cotton-wool twisted round fine forceps. A bath now and then will do no harm, but too much washing is not to be recommended because the skin will dry up and frequent baths are not necessary if the daily brushing is attended to. Whenever the dog is washed, it should be well dried, kept in a warm, draught-free place and not let out of doors until it is quite dry.

Last but not least, the most important part of the care is exercise. Dogs often get too little; like their wild ancestors they are very active, and to keep fit, bodily and mentally, they need plenty of exercise, whether they be large or small. A scantily fed dog that gets plenty of free exercise and plays a lot will be in far better condition than a dog that gets exactly the food he needs but lacks exercise. If, apart from letting it out at least three times a day, you cannot spare the time for a daily walk of no less than an hour, then you should not keep a dog. During that hour, your dog should be let off the lead in surroundings where there is no danger of accidents.

Training

Breeds of a docile nature will demand much less patience in training than the more self-willed. The strict obedience which is characteristic of the sheep-herding dog should not be expected from the hound, but all dogs can be made obedient to a degree. In order to achieve this, you should keep to the rules made for the puppy and avoid confusing yours by allowing something out of sheer laziness which is usually forbidden.

If you often go out by car it can be very useful if the dog can be taken with you. Take your dog with you often, at first only for a short time, in order to get it accustomed to the car and later on leave it alone in the car for progressively longer periods of time. See to it that the car does not stand in the sun and will not do so later, and always leave one or two windows ajar to ensure enough fresh air. If the dog is young, do not forget to give it the ox-hide ball to keep him happy. Never use the luggage compartment for transporting the dog.

The care of the sick dog

A dog cannot tell you that it is not feeling well any more than a baby can. The latter will give warning by crying, the former can only do so by a change in behaviour. The owner should pay careful attention to any unusual behaviour in the dog. If it is less lively than usual and quieter, watch it carefully; check whether the motions are normal and take its temperature. This is about 101·4°F for a healthy dog, 102°F is a high temperature and more than 102·5°F is a fever. To take the temperature, insert a greased thermometer about two inches (fifty millimetres) into the rectum. if the dog does not tolerate this easily, it should be held firmly, so as to avoid breaking the thermometer. After three minutes the temperature can be read. If symptoms of illness are apparent never try treating your dog yourself but call in the vet at once. An illness is usually cured much more quickly at an early stage than after it has been neglected for some time, so prompt action will save the owner a good deal of expense. If the dog has to take a pill or powder you should first try to see if it will swallow it well wrapped in something nice, such as a ball of minced meat. If this does not succeed, take the medicine between your fingers, open the dog's mouth, place the pill well on the back of the tongue and push it down the throat. Then close the mouth and stroke the throat, so compelling the dog to swallow. To administer a liquid medicine, the dog's head should be lifted slightly and the mouth held shut. Open the cheek at the corner of the mouth and with a spoon or a small glass, pour in the medicine; this will easily run into the mouth.

A do-it-yourself cardboard collar prevents a dog licking a wound.

As in the first case, stroke the throat and do not release the dog until he has swallowed. If the ears need treatment with powder or drops, you can without risk carefully insert a small syringe or dropper fairly deeply. With the eyes, on the other hand, you should always keep a good distance and hold the dog's head very tightly. If the dog must wear a bandage and you cannot keep a constant watch to make sure that it does not tear it off, it may be of help to sprinkle it with a liquid which keeps dogs away from bitches in heat. This liquid is also handy for separating fighting dogs. Spray a little bit on their noses and they will immediately let go; take care, however, that the spray does not get into their eyes. If a long-haired dog has dirtied himself and is too ill to be washed, you can sprinkle the spots to be cleaned with baby powder and then brush them carefully. If necessary the hair should be cut away. Always put a sick dog in a quiet, warm place.

The litter

Before deciding to breed a litter you should consider carefully what you are doing. In the first place you will be responsible for new lives. It is often no easy task to find a good home for all the puppies. Should you have misjudged a home, notwithstanding every precaution, you must be ready and able to take back the puppy and look out for a good new home. This applies too, if one of the puppies should have to change homes through unforeseen circumstances.

If whelping does not take the usual course and the bitch proves unable to take care of the litter herself, you will have to take over the task from her. It goes without saying that this will demand a great deal of work and you will lose many hours of sleep. Only if you are fully prepared to make all these sacrifices may you call yourself a serious breeder, aware of your responsibilities. It is possible to arrange for the services of a foster-mother, and an advertisement inserted in the local press or in a national dog paper will usually lead to the provision of another bitch that has whelped at the same time as yours, and which will take over the feeding of your bitch's puppies.

If you own a bitch of a certain breed and wish to raise litters, you should strive for the best possible result and try to maintain or improve the quality of the breed. Therefore it is necessary to choose a sire very carefully and if you are not very knowledgeable yourself, it is wise to consult an expert or the breed club. These will have information at their disposal enabling them to

Inserting pills and administering liquid medicines.

advise you regarding certain combinations. If this is the dam's first whelping it would be well to read a good book on the subject, where useful advice will be found.

Usually the bitch is taken to a dog for mating and the owner of the sire has the right to a stud fee or the pick of the litter. These matters can be arranged mutually. The contract should be in writing.

During her pregnancy, which lasts for about sixty-three days, the bitch will need extra nourishment. A small daily portion of raw liver is good for her. This time should be used to make all the preparations for the whelping.

A whelping box.

Measurements of the whelping-box should be one and a half times the length of the bitch lying on her side. It should be quite deep, so as to allow room to assist the dam if necessary. To make it easier for the bitch to step in and out of the box, it should be possible to turn down one of the sides. A rail is fixed along the sides of the box, several inches from the bottom and sides, depending on the size of the dam, to prevent the latter crushing her puppies between her back and the side of the box. These can be removed after two weeks. Spread a thick layer of folded newspapers on the bottom, which will make it easy to keep it constantly clean. Remember to collect a large quantity of 'reading matter' in good time! Put the box in a well-warmed place, and for the first few days out of full daylight. Let your vet know in good time that your bitch is expecting a litter.

The bitch's behaviour will show when the whelping is at hand. Some time before she may refuse food, she will be restless, start to pant and her temperature will drop to about 99°F. It is then time to lead her to the box. Usually the bitch is able to do everything herself, but she will no doubt like one of the family, to whom she is very attached, to keep her company. If you think that everything is not going normally, for instance if the time between the birth of the puppies exceeds two or three hours, then you should warn the vet. Have him examine her when the whelping has been completed; he will then check to see that no puppy has been retained within her, that the secretion of milk is sufficient and he will give any necessary injections. The bitch should be given a strengthening diet of meat, fish and eggs with special attention to sufficient cod-liver oil and calcium. Moreover she should have plenty of liquids, beef tea, milk or buttermilk and water.

At three or four weeks you may start giving the puppies extra food in the form of finely minced meat. The first day give a small ball of minced meat from which you should carefully smear a tiny bit on the puppy's tongue; it will then be greedily sucked up. The second day make it two small balls and so on up to the right amount for each breed. If the meat is readily accepted, you can start with some milk mixture. The most efficient is rice-flour, sweetened with glucose; a little cream may be added to the milk. The meals are then increased little by little.

When the puppies are four weeks old, they will try to climb over the edge of the box. The time has then come to provide them with other accommodation. The most efficient is a kennel with a large enough run to give them room for play. The floors of both should be covered with newspapers so as to make cleaning easy. From the age of four to six weeks the puppies should have access to fresh air and if possible sunshine. An enclosed space with a kennel in which to shelter from rain or too warm sun is ideal. So the moment draws near at which the prospective new owners will come to choose their puppies. All too soon they will collect them and take them to their new homes. When the whole litter has departed and everything is tidied up, an emptiness will be left behind, but also the memory of a most captivating and heart-warming experience.

Parts of the dog

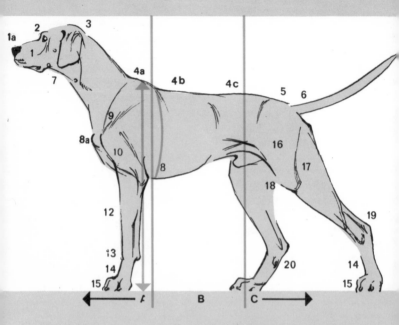

External characteristics The outward appearance of a dog consists of the forequarters (A), middle part (B) and hindquarters (C). The height at withers is measured by the perpendicular, taken from the top of the shoulders; the width of the chest is measured over the deepest point of the chest, directly under the elbow and withers (blue).

Some particular expressions are used for the parts of a dog. They are as follows: 1 muzzle, 1a nose, 2 stop, 3 occiput, 4 back, 4a withers, 4b back, 4c loin (seen from above) and coupling (seen from the side), 5 croup, (4a, 4b, 4c and 5 together are called topline), 6 tail root, 7 cheek- and throat wart, 8 chest, 8a breastbone, 8b forechest, 8c brisket or lower chest, 9 shoulder, 10 upper arm, 11 elbow, 12 forearm, 13 wrist or pastern joint, 14 front pastern, 15 forefoot or paw, 16 upper thigh, 17 second thigh or gaskin, 18 knee or stifle, 19 hock joint or point of hock, 20 dewclaws. This dew claw does not exist with all breeds; very often it is removed by operation. However, some French sheep-herding breeds even have two dewclaws on the same spot which is demanded by the breed standards.

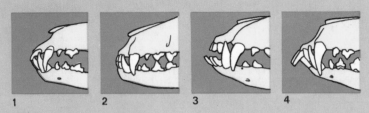

The teeth of a dog are not the same for all breeds. Regarding the placing of the incisors, the following terms are used: **1 scissor bite,** top teeth (incisors) just overlapping the lower (like a pair of scissors); **2 level bite,** teeth (incisors) meeting evenly, edge to edge; **3 undershot bite,** the lower jaw protruding further than the upper jaw; **4 overshot bite,** upper front teeth projecting beyond the lower (this is always a fault).

The head can differ from the general type, in a number of ways: **1 down-faced,** nasal bone sloping downwards to the nostrils; **2 dish-faced,** concavity of line of head, dish-shaped; **3 cheeky,** having thick, protruding cheek muzzles (masseter); **4 scowl,** the frown of a Chow Chow; **5 peak,** a well-developed occiput; **6 square muzzle.**

The eyes can show the following peculiarities: **a wall eyes,** or china-eyes, with a blue iris; **b hawk eyes,** a yellow eye, usually not preferable because of the harsh and cold staring expression; **c haw,** an inner eyelid or membrane at inside corner.

29

The ears of the original breeds have a triangular, moderately tapering shape; with the domestic breeds we speak of a **fox ear** (inset). **1** The normal prick ear of the domestic breeds is usually bigger and more pointed. **2** A curious ear shape we find with the French Bulldog, the **tulip** or **bat ear**, is an erect open ear, broad at base, tulip shaped, rounded at top.

Next to the erect ear are many shapes of the ear with half erect and hanging variations. **3** The **semi-prick ear** (of the Collie and Shetland Sheepdog, for example) is very striking; when the tip of the ear is not drooping we call it a **prick ear. 4** The **button ear** is an ear with a flap folding forwards covering the orifice and the tip pointing towards the eye. **5** The **drop ear** hangs flat and close to the cheeks; the ears of some gundogs (3, below) are lower, sit further back to the skull, and are turned in like a screw. **6** The **lobular shaped ear** is a variation the Cocker Spaniel has.

The **rose shaped ears** (1, below) are ears which are small, thin, and folded inwards at the back (some hounds, like Borzoi, Greyhound, Whippet). The **cropping** (ears trimmed in puppyhood to stand erect) of ears is forbidden by law in some countries and in others the exhibition of dogs with cropped ears is not permissible under kennel club regulations.

The neck is judged by the way the skin fits, as follows: **1 dry**, when the skin fits tightly and is well-muscled; **2 throaty**, when there is excessive loose skin at the throat; **3 dewlap**, when there is loose pendulous skin under the throat.

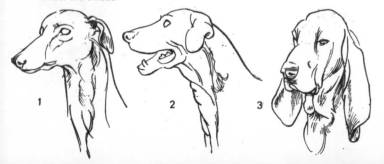

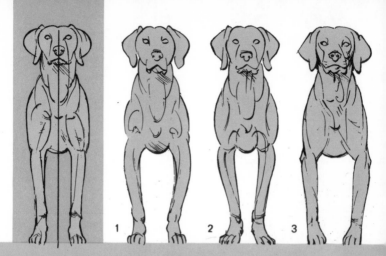

The forequarters of most breeds show a straight front (inset). Rickets, mistreatment during the growing period and insufficient nourishment can cause undesirable bends: **1 out at elbow**, outwards bent underarm; **2 fiddle front**, a faulty front for many breeds, the feet are turned outwards; **3 loose elbows**, the elbows are turned outwards and the feet inwards. This is often caused by frequently picking up the puppy at his elbows. Some breeds of hounds have a straight front with the feet slightly turned inwards and this is a typical and normal front for them.

The hindquarters generally have the same requirements as for the forequarters; they should be correct and straight, seen from behind. **1 barrel-hocked hindquarters**; **2 cow-hocked**, very often inherited; **3 narrow hindquarters**, a fault which becomes obvious when the dog is in movement.

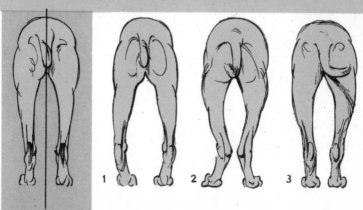

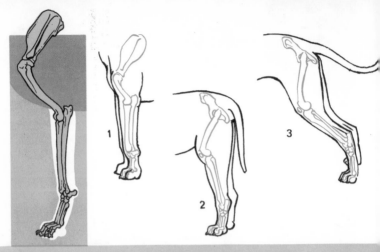

The legs must be regarded with their function in mind — i.e. as a mechanism to aid movement. Studying the legs from top to bottom it seems that the different parts always vary in direction. This is due to the law of balance and gravity, which dictates an efficient forward motion with a minimum waste of effort. **1** and **2 A straight front** or **straight stifled hindquarters** will make movement bumpy and the step too short; **3 well-angulated hindquarters** (as well as stifle joint and hock) are necessary for a sound driving movement.

The feet. Dogs belong to the digitigrade which means that only the toes (phalanges) touch the ground. The phalanges are bedded in the communal pad and the individual foot pads. The shape of the foot can vary: **1 cat foot**, short, round and compact; **2 hare foot**, an elongated oval foot; **3 splay foot**, this is a fault (the figure shows the right forefoot, the fifth phalange [dewclaw] is often taken away shortly after birth).

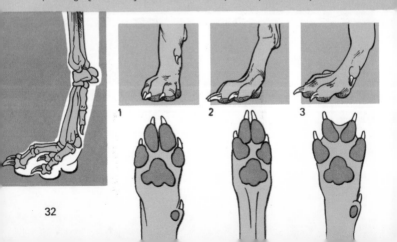

The tail shows more variations than any other part of the dog. Quite apart from the differences in length, natural and by docking, the shape varies with the way in which it is carried, the amount and direction of bend and the amount of coat.

Ways of tail carriage: **a** low; **b** below the topline; **c** level with the topline; **d** above topline; **e** and **f** gay; **g** over the back.

Ways of bending: **1 sword tail**, almost straight, long and low-set; **2 sabre tail**, high set, slightly bent upwards; **3 sickle tail**, bent further upwards; **4 ringtail**, tail which curves in a circle; **5 tailcurl**, the end of the tail is curled like a ring (Afghan); **6 hooked tail**, the end of the tail forms a hook; **7 spiral tail**, carried with a double curl over the upper thigh (Wetterhorn); **8 curled tail**, tightly curled over the back; **9 twisted tail**, double curl as tightly as possible over the hip (Pug); **10 screw tail**, as in a French Bulldog. Coat and feathers are essential for the following tails: **11 plume tail**, having a long fringe of hairs; **12 ottertail**, thick tapering tail, hairs very thick and short (Labrador Retriever); **13 brushed** (or **fox**) **tail**, well-covered with hair and bushy (Siberian Husky).

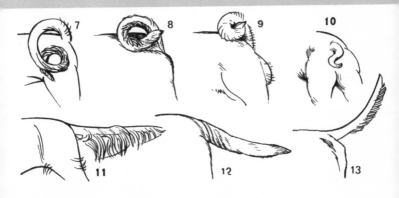

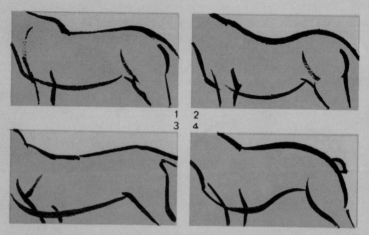

The back can differ in a number of ways. Two faults are: **1 a dip in the back** and **2 a hollow back**. The following deviations are accepted in some breeds: **3** being **overbuilt** (the croup is higher than the withers); **4 a roach back** rises over the loin and curves down to the tail as in the Bulldog, Bedlington Terrier and some greyhounds.

The coat shows, from the effects of domestication, a great variety. The original coat is a **double smooth** coat, a woolly thick and close undercoat; the outercoat is also close, each hair straight, hard and lying flat. There are **short, smooth** coats (1–2 inches) and **long, smooth** coats (3–5 inches). A short coat is fine, short, soft and glossy. A **wire-haired** coat feels harsh and points in all directions, often combined with bushy muzzle and eyebrows; this coat can differ in length (rough-haired German Pointer—short; wire-haired German Pointer—long).
1 The Rhodesian Ridgeback has a ridge on the back which is formed by the hair growing in the opposite direction to the rest of the coat. 2 Coats with very long silky uppercoats always go together with feathering (a long fringe of hairs). 3 Heavy coats go with a mane and culotte.

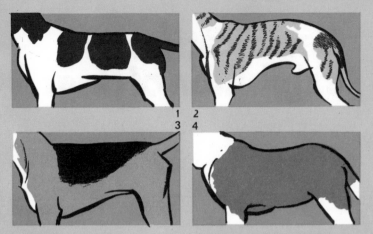

The colour is described by a variety of terms: **1 plates,** large patches on a lighter background; **2 brindle,** definite dark stripes on a pale background; **3 saddle,** saddle-shaped dark marking on the back; **4 mantle,** the dark portion of the coat, on shoulders, back and sides. Other often used terms are: **trace,** a black line extending from the occiput to the twist; **blue merle,** a silvery blue, splashed and dappled with black, tan and white markings; **harlequin,** white dog usually with black or blue irregular markings; **isabella,** a light straw or fawn colour; **tan,** a rusty colour. Furthermore, there are terms such as badger coloured, fawn, sable, apricot, mustard, pepper and wheaten, which refer to the colouring of these plants and animals.

Markings, occurring symmetrically on head, chest, and legs are called: **1 chest cross; 2 blaze; 3 mask; 4 kissmarks** (the cheek markings of a black and tan pattern); **5 eye patch.**

Classification and exhibition of dogs

Breed groupings

Grouping differs from one country to another; in some it is arranged by type, in some by country of origin and in others according to the work that a dog does, or its purpose. At one time the simplest form of division was probably adopted, that is, dogs were divided into working dogs and non-working dogs, but as the number of breeds increased, the groups formed by this sort of division became unwieldly. Subsequently the working group would probably have been divided into herding dogs, dogs of the chase and guard dogs, whilst the non-working group would become a single group composed of all the others. This in its turn would again become unwieldly, and the dogs that were purely companions would be divided into large companion dogs and small companion dogs, resulting in what are now known in Britain as the utility group and the toy group. There would always remain shadowy areas in which certain breeds that had ceased to be bred for a specific purpose owing to changes in human habits, would be difficult to place. The Bulldog, for instance, which ceased to work when bull-baiting became illegal.

This type of division has developed over the years into a convention for arranging the various breeds of dogs into groups for the purpose of exhibition. There still remain a large number of breeds that are bred for work, or purely for the purpose of retaining a type, and these are either not normally exhibited, or become involved in the fringe area between regular exhibition and an occasional appearance as a rare breed.

There will be breeds listed in this book that the average reader will not have heard of, let alone seen; breeds that exist in very small numbers or in a very restricted area. Some have survived as the result of the efforts of a single breeder and some have been created but never achieved popularity. The fact remains that it is only through exhibition that any breed of dog becomes known. This is where the exhibition of dogs ceases to be purely a hobby, or a personal pursuit of profit or enjoyment and becomes educational. It is not so many years since the uninformed person's idea of a giraffe was very odd indeed. So odd that it was known as a Cameleopard and visualized as a most peculiar beast until it appeared for the first time in public. Breeds such as the Komondor, though known in America and seen regularly on the Continent, had not been seen in Great Britain until very recently and few people will have seen one, even among regular showgoers.

It will probably therefore be simpler to deal with the question of the grouping of the various breeds of dogs on the basis of exhibition rather than upon any arrangement based upon size, type, or country of origin. The spitz group is not recognized under the British and American way of thinking, as breeds from this group appear under several headings in both countries; similarly the Pomeranian in the toy group, the Chow Chow in the utility group and the Elkhound in the hound group, to quote a few examples.

In Britain, the Kennel Club is satisfied to divide the breeds into six groups—hound, terrier, toy, gundog, working and utility—and in practice this now works out fairly well, with approximately the same number of breeds in each group. In America the groups are: sporting, hound, working, terrier, toy and non-sporting, where again the numbers of breeds work out at roughly the same. Under a system of judging a show in which the various breeds are shown as a group, with a best of group being decided upon, and only the winners of the group going forward to the final best in show competition, this equal division of the breeds is important. A fault that existed in Britain at one time was that in one group of best of breed winners there were a large number of dogs, whilst in another group there were considerably fewer. This has now been eradicated.

In other countries the number of groups and the arrangement of breeds within those groups differ considerably. In Italy, for instance, the introduction of the bassotti as a group, the division of gundogs into native breeds and English gundogs, and the severance of the levrieri or running dogs from the hound group, has resulted in the formation of ten groups. In Sweden, because of their greater number of breeds of this type, the spitz dogs became a separate group, and the vinthunden or coursing dogs were separated from the hunting dog group, resulting in eight groups. Some countries, such as Australia, have adopted the British standards *en bloc*, whilst others tend to follow the standards laid down by the American Kennel Club.

Hence it can be seen that the grouping of dogs generally follows the same basic pattern world-wide, but that variations occur from country to country. This book has been compiled by an European expert, with the breeds grouped in the Continental way as follows:

Sheep-herding dogs	Gundogs
Guard and utility dogs	Large companion dogs
Terriers	Small companion dogs
Hounds and greyhounds	

Ruling bodies

National kennel clubs are the guiding bodies in their respective countries for all canine affairs. They are responsible for the registration of dogs, societies and councils and for the administration of canine affairs as they affect societies wishing to organize shows. They make rules and regulations and are responsible for discipline and conduct. They act as clearing houses for information, publishers of documents concerning breeders, owners and exhibitors, advisers to everyone interested in dogs and dog shows, as well as of all other canine activities such as obedience and field trials. They are accepted, in their own country, as the ruling body on all matters concerning dogs.

In addition there is one very important international body, the Fédération Cynologique Internationale, which now wields a great deal of influence in many countries throughout the world; countries as far apart as Scandinavia and South America. This body is not so much a kennel club or council as a federation of a large number of such clubs and councils. For a while its influence was centred around Europe, but in recent years it has spread further afield and many of the newer national bodies that are set up, seek to join it. The work that it does is varied and does have a good deal of influence on the thinking of many countries, particularly those that have not over the years built up a very strong national body.

Its influence is most obvious in the particular title that it awards to outstanding dogs. In countries that have their own national bodies, a dog may become a champion, a title which it can then proudly carry. The methods by which this is done vary from country to country. In Britain a dog becomes a champion by winning three Challenge Certificates under three different approved judges, one of the Certificates having been awarded after the dog has become twelve months of age. Other countries have a points system, or special conditions about when, where and by whom the Certificates are awarded.

The Fédération Cynologique Internationale permits member national bodies to award, under certain circumstances, the C.A.C.I.B., which is the FCI's certificate, which will help that dog to be granted the title of International Champion. Many dogs are called International Champions when they have gained the award of Champion in more than one country, but the FCI maintain that the only true International Champion is the one that has been awarded the title under its regulations.

In addition to this rather detailed involvement in canine affairs, the FCI holds regular International Conferences in different countries around the world, at which a good deal of very serious discussion takes place. There has been a move in recent years towards better understanding between the various national bodies that govern dogs and dog shows, particularly over the question of breed standards, and the FCI has been one of the principal advocates of this. At present breed standards vary from country to country, mostly in matters of detail, but there is a certain amount of variation in such things as colour and size which can lead to confusion. Nowadays, when a new breed is imported into a country, the newly formed breed club of that country adopts the breed standard of the country of origin. This has not always happened in the past with the result that there has been a certain friction about dogs that have been re-exported.

Show dogs

Whichever country one happens to be resident in, the guiding body in all matters concerned with registering, naming and exhibiting dogs will be the kennel club or council of that country.

Once a puppy has reached the age at which it may be exhibited —and here again this varies from country to country, six months in Britain, three months in Australia—it may be entered and shown at any dog show or in any classes from which by age or achievement it is not barred.

Most newcomers to dog showing will begin at a smaller show in order to gain experience and at this type of show, as at most, the classes are arranged in such a way that a young and inexperienced dog will be in competition with dogs of similar age and lack of show experience. This means that unless a puppy does extremely well before it reaches adulthood, it will usually find itself in a class to which it is suited and will not be in competition with really big winners.

Kennel clubs throughout the world have their own ways of dividing the inexperienced dogs from the experienced, and their regulations will contain the basic divisions of classification into age groups, and will in addition have regulations governing what is a Novice and a Tyro, and when a dog has reached the stage at which it becomes a Graduate. All the information concerning this is contained in regulations of the definitions of classes.

Most shows throughout the world, particularly at championship level, are divided by groups so that dogs of the same breed will not only compete against each other, but will at the next stage compete against others of the same group, so that gundogs will compete against gundogs and terriers against terriers and so on. It is only in the final stages of a show that the representatives of the groups will meet one another when they line up to compete for the supreme award of best in show.

In the smaller shows in Britain, there are also other classes called 'variety classes' that consist of exhibits that are bred by the exhibitor, or those that belong to a lady or similar arbitary divisions that have nothing to do with the age or attainment of the dog itself.

What are called groups in other countries at shows, are often not what is generally understood as a division in Britain or America, but are in fact often families of dogs; sometimes dogs all sired by the same stud dog or dogs all belonging to the same exhibitor and exhibited together and competing against similar small groups of dogs shown by other exhibitors. This sort of class causes considerable interest, especially in Scandinavian shows, where they are a very popular feature because the ring appears to be full of dogs.

Working dogs

Dogs are not just bred for show. Many breeders concentrate on the working qualities, and have as their first consideration the temperament and ability to perform the duties that the breed was developed for. The Alsatian, or German Shepherd Dog, is a typical example of this. A large number are bred for the show ring, but many more are bred from stock that has proved itself in the obedience ring for the purpose of competing in obedience classes, the vast majority of the dogs competing in such classes being in fact dogs of this breed. The German Shepherd Dog is a typical example of a dog reaching great heights of popularity because of its multi-purpose qualities. They are first rate show dogs, excellent obedience competitors, very good guard and police dogs and have a tremendous sale as pets.

There are many breeds that have for years been bred for work, and have only in recent years been shown at dog shows, partly to bring them before the public and partly because a small number of owners realized their potential in this direction. The Maremma is a typical example of this. Bred as a working dog in central Italy, it was suddenly appreciated that here was a dog of striking appearance and great tractability, which would make a good show dog. This it has proved and examples of the breed are now seen in the show-ring of a good many countries.

At one time the hills and pastures, forests and woodlands of their native countries were the proving grounds of most breeds of dogs, but there has been a great swing round towards the exhibiting of dogs, and the show ring is now the proving ground and the development area. Many breeds owe their continued existence to the dog show and the future of the dog, which is the most domesticated of all animals, lies undoubtedly in its continued improvement for exhibition purposes.

H.G.

Descriptions
of breeds

Sheep-herding dogs

This group includes all those breeds which have developed from dogs that, for thousands of years, have helped herdsmen with their cattle and sheep. They can be subdivided into mountain dogs (the oldest breeds of this group) and shepherd or sheepdogs.

The nomadic shepherd tribes adopted mountain dogs as guards to warn them of the approach of beasts of prey and to protect them and their herds. These dogs needed to be large, strong, courageous and preferably white, so that in the dark the shepherd who came to their assistance could distinguish them from bears and wolves. All these breeds of mountain dogs carry a strain of Mastiff blood, the fighting dog of old. When these tribes gradually abandoned their wandering life and settled down to raising crops and breeding animals, the need developed for dogs which kept the herds together and prevented them from trampling over the fields. Dogs were then bred which were more suited to this work than the heavy and rather cumbersome mountain dogs. The lighter and more mobile animals which were obtained are thought to be the ancestors of our present-day shepherd and sheepdogs. In the countries where nomadic shepherds still wander with their herds, one or two of these dogs remain their much valued assistants.

Few of these working breeds are ever found outside their native countries or seen at shows. Any successful herd dog must have the instinct to control a large group of cattle, keep them together, be able quickly to understand the directions of the shepherd and be intelligent enough to take the necessary initiative. The last two qualities are especially required in order to keep together a grazing herd on the move. Moreover, the dog should be able to guard and defend the shepherd and the flock. Sheepdogs have been selectively bred for centuries to strengthen these characteristics, and they are still to be found in all sheepdog breeds, making them dogs particularly responsive to all kinds of training. They are not only good guards of house and home and defenders of their owner and his family, but very fit for police work, as guide dogs for finding lost people in the snow and even for use in tracing drugs and gas-leaks. A certain amount of pugnacity is part of their character and is necessary if they are to be used for police work and as watch-dogs and defenders. A dog who refuses to attack a man is unfit for this work. Sheep-herding dogs are trustworthy, provided you are able to handle and master them. They are definitely not suitable for nervous people. It is a mistake for such people to keep a potentially vicious dog as a protection against burglars and intruders, because without proper control they can be dangerous.

Mountain and sheep-herding dogs do not require any special grooming treatment, with the exception of a few breeds such as the Komondor and the Puli. These dogs have a special structure of thick hair and undercoat which makes the two felt. This process is quite different from the burring of long hair which occurs whenever any long-coated dog is badly groomed. In the adult dogs the coat consists of large wads or narrow strips of matted hair, the so-called felted hair. For working dogs this coat provides a thorough protection against all weather and lends them a characteristic and very typical appearance. The special property of this coat is not always appreciated and the felting is prevented by combing and brushing the coat and even using hair-spray. In this way the hair is made to stand away from the body giving the dogs a quite different appearance from that which their working kinsmen show in their original condition. In the countries of origin this unnatural mode of grooming is never applied, not even to show dogs. Any fears that without such treatment the dog would become dirty and smell unpleasant are entirely groundless. The felted white coat can easily be kept clean by parting the wads with the fingers and dividing them in long thin hanks, a natural grooming carried out by thorns and tree-branches while the dog is at work. In this way light and air are admitted, allowing the hair and skin to breathe. Moreover, the dogs can be washed if necessary. In their native Hungary they are bathed once a year and only in summer, because the coat takes a very long time to dry.

Scale of Sheep-herding dog illustrations 1 :15

1 Groenendaeler (Groenendael)

Origin descended from a mating of black, long-haired sheepdogs. He got his name from Groenendael, a castle in the forest south of Brussels.

Appearance Head long without exaggeration and moderately broad, the muzzle somewhat longer than the skull; the stop is slight. **Eyes** almond-shaped, preferably dark brown with a bold, intelligent and inquiring expression. **Ears** triangular prick ears. **Neck** rather long and without throatiness. **Body** deep but not too broad. **Legs** medium length and strong. **Feet** almost round, the hind feet more oval. **Tail** of moderate length. **Coat** short on the head, the ears and the front of the legs, long on the body and longer still around the neck and on the back of the legs and the tail.

Character robust, intelligent, lively, good watch-dog, responsive to training.

2 Laekense (Laeken)

Origin and use neighbourhood of Boom, near Antwerp, where many bleach-works were established and the dogs were used to guard the fields where costly linen was put out to bleach.

Appearance similar to that of the Groenendael, except for the **colour**, which should be fawn with blackening on the muzzle and tail; and the **coat**, which should be rough, harsh, shaggy and 2½ inches (6cm) long, except on the head, which is short-haired.

3 Mechelaar (Malinois)

Origin and use the Campine country and the north of Brabant where they are used as drovers for cattle and sheep. The name comes from the town of Mechelen (Malines).

Appearance similar to the Groenendael, except for the **coat**, which is dense and short, somewhat longer on neck and tail, and the **colour**.

1
Height at withers:
dog: about 24½ inches
(62 cm), bitch: about
23 inches (58 cm).
Colour: black.

2
Height at withers:
dog: about 24½ inches
(62 cm), bitch: about
23 inches (58 cm).
Colour: fawn with
traces of black on
muzzle.

3
Height at withers:
dog: about 24½ inches
(62 cm), bitch: about
23 inches (58 cm).
Colour: fawn with
black tips, preferably
with black mask.

4 Tervuerense (Tervuren)

Origin Tervuren, near Brussels. Same descent as that of the Groenendael.
Appearance similar to that of the Groenendael, except the **colour**, which should be rich fawn with the tip of each hair black, with the face-mark and ears largely black and a black tip to the tail.

5 Berger de Beauce (Beauceron)

Origin surprisingly, not the region of Beauce but of Brie.
Appearance Head long with little stop, the skull and muzzle are of the same length. **Eyes** dark or harmonizing with the colour of the coat. **Ears** may be cropped or natural; the former is preferred in countries where cropping is permitted. **Neck** moderately long. **Body** a deep chest. **Legs** strong and of medium length; the hind legs have double dew claws. **Feet** round. **Coat** black and not too short, a little less than an inch (2 cm) thick; it lies close to the body.
Character intelligent, obedient, calm, fierce if necessary, very responsive to training.

6 Berger de Brie (Briard)

Origin the name probably has nothing to do with the region of Brie but is a corruption of 'Chien d'Aubry'. In 1317 a dog of the type is reported to have traced the murderer of his master, a nobleman named Aubry de Montdidier. The Briard is found all over France, especially in the north and appears to be descended from the Barbet and Beauceron.
Appearance Head not too broad and sufficiently long, with marked stop. **Eyes** rather large and dark, with a calm, intelligent expression. **Ears** preferably cropped in countries where this is permitted and if not, short and not too drooping. **Neck** rather long, **Body** a broad, deep chest. **Legs** rather long with strong bone; the hind legs have double dew claws. **Feet** between hare- and catfeet. **Tail** moderately long with a hook at the tip. **Coat** long, harsh and not lying close to the body, any solid colour except white.
Character lively, happy, intelligent, easily offended.

4
Height at withers:
dog: about 24½ inches
(62 cm), bitch: about
23 inches (58 cm).
Colour: reddish fawn
with sable sheen,
preferably with black
mask.

5
Height at withers:
dog: 26½ inches
(67 cm), bitch: 25½
inches (65 cm).
Colour: black, black
and tan, fawn, fawn
with dark tips, grey,
grey with black spots.

6
Height at withers:
dog: 23–27 inches
(58½–68½ cm),
bitch: 22–26 inches
(56–66 cm).
Colour: all colours
except white, always
self-coloured,
preferably dark
colours.

7 Berger de l'Atlas (Berger d'Algérie, Aïda, Chien Kabyle, Chien des Douars, Algerian Sheepdog)

Origin and use a native of the Kabyle Mountains and common as a hill-shepherd's dog in Tunisia and Algeria, where they guard the tent villages of the Arabs, called douars, and herd the cattle. Their popularity would perhaps be greater, were it not for their ferocious nature.

Appearance Head rather long, with slight stop and long muzzle. **Eyes** dark, with an intelligent, lively expression. **Ears** triangular prick ears. **Neck** rather strong. **Feet** oval. **Tail** long and well furnished. **Coat** close to the body and not too short, coarse and stiff.

Character ferocious, unfriendly, watchful.

8 Berger de Picardie (Picard)

Origin and use the north of France. Probably the oldest French sheep-herding dog, the breed is thought to have been brought to France by the Celts in the ninth century. It is still a working dog, not a show dog.

Appearance Head a rather broad, slightly arched skull, a slight stop and not too long muzzle. **Eyes** medium sized and dark. **Ears** not too large, prick ears. **Neck** not too short. **Body** moderately long and has a deep, not too broad chest. **Legs** of medium length with good bone. **Feet** round. **Tail** long. **Coat** hard and half long, should feel rough to the touch and has a dense undercoat.

Character fierce, pugnacious, untiring, faithful, affectionate, good with children.

9 Berger des Pyrénées (Pyrenean Sheepdog)

Origin the whole area of the Pyrenees, from Cerdogne to far into the Landes. Originated by crossing indigenous dogs with Briards and Beaucerons who brought their flocks there.

Appearance Head a rather flat skull, no visible stop and a not heavy, short muzzle. **Eyes** chestnut, but wall eyes or eyes with blue spots are permissible for white, black and grey dogs. **Ears** drop ears, preferably cropped rather short. **Neck** rather long. **Body** long with slightly arched ribs; the breast reaches to the elbow. **Legs** dry and not heavy; the hind legs may have single or double dew claws. **Feet** oval. **Tail** long with a hook at the tip; both natural short tail or docked tail are allowed. **Coat** long or medium long, lying close to the body or slightly wavy.

Character highly strung, distrustful, very lively and intelligent, good watch-dog.

10 Berger des Pyrénées à face rase (Pyrenean Sheepdog with short-haired face)

Origin and use same as that of the Pyrenean Sheepdog.

Appearance similar to that of the Pyrenean Sheepdog except the **head** which has a longer and more pointed muzzle, and the **coat** which is medium long and short on the head and the fronts of the legs.

7

Height at withers:
22–24 inches
(56–61 cm).
Colour: white,
sometimes with fawn
marks. Dark colours
seldom occur.

8

Height at withers:
dog: 24–26 inches
(61–66 cm), bitch:
22–24 inches
(56–61 cm).
Colour: grey, grey-
black, grey-blue,
grey-red, light and
dark fawn without
white. Only white toes
and spot on the breast
are allowed.

9

Height at withers:
dog: 16–20 inches
(40½–51 cm), bitch:
15–20 inches
(38–51 cm).
Colour: reddish, grey,
patched, black with
white markings on
head, breast and feet.

11 Bouvier des Ardennes (Ardennes Cattle Dog)

Origin and use the Belgian Ardennes, where it is still frequently used with cattle. Its looks are more those of a sheep-herding dog than of a cattle dog. It is not a show dog.

Appearance Head heavy and moderately short with slight stop. **Eyes** dark. **Ears** should be prick ears but tip ears are permissible. **Neck** short and thick. **Body** of medium length with a deep and broad chest. **Legs** of medium length and heavily boned. **Feet** round. **Tail** docked very short. **Coat** shaggy and harsh, about 2 inches (5 cm) long, shorter on head and legs. In winter it has a thick undercoat. There are whiskers and a beard on the muzzle.

Character intelligent, willing to please his master, surly to strangers.

12 Bouvier de Flandre (Belgian Cattle Dog)

Origin and use the French–Belgian frontier country, where presumably the Chien de Berger Picard and the Mâtin Belge were its ancestors. Originally used for many purposes such as a cattle drover, a guard, a watch-dog and even as a draught-dog.

Appearance Head a rather wide and flat skull, a slight stop and a short, broad muzzle. **Eyes** dark and oval with a bold expression. **Ears** generally cropped and not too long. **Neck** not too short and without throatiness. **Body** short and deep. **Legs** medium long with strong bone. **Feet** round. **Tail** docked to about 4 inches (10 cm). **Coat** rough and slightly shaggy, about 2½ inches (6 cm) long.

Character intelligent, lively, energetic, brave, responsive to training.

13 Cane da Pastore Bergamasco (Bergamaschi, Bergama Sheepdog)

Origin the mountains in the north of Italy. The great similarity with the Briard suggests the same ancestry.

Appearance Head a broad, slightly arched skull, pronounced stop and square, not too long muzzle. **Eyes** dark; blue eyes are allowed for light-coloured dogs. **Ears** small and semi-pricked. **Neck** rather long. **Body** of moderate length with sufficiently arched ribs. **Legs** fairly long and strong. **Feet** round. **Tail** of medium length. **Coat** long, somewhat wavy and woolly, harsh on the back.

Character courageous, trustworthy, good watch-dog.

11

Height at withers:
medium size: 24 inches
(61 cm) at most, large
size: at least 24 inches
(61 cm).
Colour: all colours
permissible.

12

Height at withers:
dog: 26 inches
(66 cm), bitch: 25
inches (63½ cm).
Colour: from drab
yellow to black, grey,
brindle.

13

Height at withers:
dog: about 24 inches
(61 cm), bitch: about
22 inches (56 cm).
Colour: grey in every
shade, with or without
white or black spots or
mingled with yellow
or brown.

14 Cane da Pastore Maremmano (Abruzzese, Maremma Sheepdog)

Origin and use popular in Italy as a working sheep-herding dog it was probably introduced by Magyars arriving from Asia. The mountain dogs from the Maremma and the Abruzzi were considered different breeds until 1958, since when they have been recognized as a single breed.

Appearance Head recalls that of a white bear. The skull is rather broad and long, the muzzle is slightly shorter and strong, medium stop. **Eyes** not large, almond-shaped and brown. **Ears** small, V-shaped drop ears. **Neck** strong, without throatiness. **Body** moderately long with broad and deep chest. **Legs** of medium length, large in bone. **Feet** oval. **Coat** profuse, long and rather hard, but short on head and foreside of legs which are slightly feathered.

15 Cão da Serra de Aires (Portuguese Sheepdog)

Origin and use originated from old indigenous sheep-herding dogs in Portugal. They are used as herding dogs.

Appearance Head rather broad, with marked stop and strong, not too short muzzle. **Eyes** brown. **Ears** drop ears, often cropped. **Neck** not too short. **Body** rather long with deep chest. **Legs** strong and of medium length. **Feet** oval. **Tail** long. **Coat** very long, smooth or slightly wavy.

Character active, intelligent, tough.

16 Collie, Bearded

Origin a document dated 1514 records that traders from Poland bringing sheep to exchange for Scottish sheep, brought three Polish Lowland Sheepdogs on their ships, a dog and two bitches, which were bartered for a ram and a ewe. Those dogs might be the first ancestors of the Bearded Collie.

Appearance Head a broad, flat skull, slight stop and rather long muzzle. **Eyes** in harmony with the colour of the coat. **Ears** moderately large drop ears. **Neck** rather long. **Body** rather long with well-sprung ribs and deep chest. **Legs** moderately long with good bone. **Feet** oval. **Tail** of moderate length. **Coat** the top coat is long, harsh and flat, the undercoat is dense and soft.

Character intelligent, affectionate, untiring, very energetic, good with children.

14

Height at withers:
dog: 26–29 inches
(66–74 cm), bitch:
24–27 inches
(61–68½ cm).
Colour: white.

15

Height at withers:
dog: 17–19 inches
(43–48½ cm), bitch:
16–18 inches
(40½–45½ cm).
Colour: yellow,
chestnut, fawn, grey,
wolf-sable, black. Tan
markings allowed.

16

Height at withers:
dog: 20–24 inches
(51–61 cm), bitch:
18–22 inches
(46–56 cm).
Colour: slate blue or
reddish cinnamon,
black, all shades of
grey, brown, sandy,
with or without
Collie markings.

17 Collie, Rough

Origin and use a very old breed from Scotland where it was used in the Highlands and Lowlands as a sheepdog.

Appearance Head a flat and moderately wide skull, a very slight stop, the muzzle being as long as the skull. **Eyes** of medium size, almond-shaped and dark brown, unless the dog has a blue merle coat, in which case the eyes may be blue or blue flecked. **Ears** small tip ears. **Neck** fairly long. **Body** rather long and has well-sprung ribs and a deep, rather broad chest. **Legs** moderately strong bone. **Feet** oval. **Tail** long. **Coat** straight, dense, hard and long on top, dense and soft underneath with a full mane, apron and brush. The head is short-haired as is the front of the legs and feet.

Character dignified, faithful, honest, intelligent, reserved with strangers.

18 Collie, Smooth

Appearance like the Rough Collie in all respects except the **coat**, which should be short, harsh and smooth.

19 Deutscher Schäferhund (German Shepherd Dog, Alsatian)

Origin and use the German forerunners of the breed were descended from animals used to protect flocks of sheep against wolves. White dogs were originally selected so that they would not be noticed among the sheep, but white, part white and cream are not favoured today.

Appearance Head a moderately broad skull, slight stop and long muzzle. **Eyes** almond-shaped, preferably dark, and have a lively and intelligent expression. **Ears** large prick ears. **Neck** of medium length without throatiness. **Body** a deep but not too broad chest with slightly arched ribs. **Legs** strongly boned and not too long. **Feet** short and round. **Tail** reaches to the hock. **Coat** dense, straight, hard, lying close to the body.

Character attentive, lively, faithful, good watch-dog, responsive to very diverse training.

17

Height at withers:
dog: 22–24 inches
(56–61 cm), bitch:
22–22 inches
(51–56 cm).
Colour: sable with
white, tricolour, blue
merle or white in USA.
In Britain any colours
and markings are
acceptable.

18

Height at withers:
dog: 22–24 inches
(55–60 cm), bitch:
20–22 inches
(50–55 cm).
Colour: sand coloured
with white, tricolour,
blue merle.

19

Height at withers:
dog: 24–26 inches
(61–66 cm), bitch:
22–24 inches
(56–61 cm).
Colour: solid black,
iron grey, grizzle, or
these colours with
brown, yellow to
grizzly white markings,
or wolf-colour.

20 Deutscher Schafpudel (German Sheep Poodle)

Origin and use Germany, where it is kept exclusively for work with the flocks.

Appearance Head a broad skull, little stop and a not too long, deep muzzle. Eyes large and dark brown. Ears rather long drop ears. Neck without throatiness. Body not too long, with well-sprung ribs and deep chest. Legs rather long. Feet strong. Tail long. Coat long, hard and shaggy.

Character intelligent, attentive, gentle, affectionate, tolerant, good watch-dog.

21 Gos d'Atura (Catalan Sheepdog)

Origin and use the Spanish Province of Catalonia. The Pyrenean Mountain Dog may be one of its ancestors. Used for droving as well as herding cattle and nowadays often employed as a watch-dog and trained for police and military work.

Appearance Head a broad skull, marked stop and strong, rather short muzzle. Eyes large, dark amber. Ears drop ears. Neck short and massive. Body of medium length with deep chest and slightly arched ribs. Legs of medium length and with heavy bone. Feet large and oval. Tail long and curled, or docked to 4 inches (10 cm). Coat long and slightly wavy.

Character reliable, eager to learn, good watch-dog.

22 Gos d'Atura Cerdà (Smooth Catalan Sheepdog)

Appearance Similar to that of the Gos d'Atura, except for the **coat**, which is rather short, soft and dense.

23 Hollandse Herdershond (Dutch Shepherd Dog short-haired)

Origin and use occurred first in those provinces of the Netherlands where many sheep were kept, especially from Brenthe to Brabant. It is very like the Belgian Shepherd Dogs. Barely seen outside Holland it is very popular there and used for police work, retrieving and as a guide dog.

Appearance Head narrow and of medium length, the skull flat, the stop scarcely apparent and the muzzle slightly longer than the skull. Eyes moderately large, almond-shaped and dark. Ears small prick ears. Neck not too short and without throatiness. Body rather short with not too narrow deep chest and slightly arched ribs. Legs of medium length and strong in bone. Feet rather short. Tail long. Coat rather hard and not too short, with woolly undercoat, with a collar and breeches of longer hair.

Character intelligent, diligent, faithful, good watch-dog, responsive to training.

20

Height at withers:
dog: 20–24 inches
(50–60 cm), bitch:
20–22 inches
(51–56 cm).
Colour: white. Roan
and pied allowed.

21

Height at withers:
dog: 18–20 inches
(45½–51 cm), bitch:
17–19 inches
(43–48½ cm).
Colour: black and
tan, black,
brindle, tan
and fawn.

23

Height at withers:
dog: 23–25 inches
(58½–65½ cm), bitch:
21½–24½ inches
(54½–62½ cm).
Colour: grey.
blue-grey.

24 Hollandse Herdershond (Dutch Shepherd Dog long-haired)

Appearance identical to that of the short-haired variety, except for the **coat** which is long, straight and rough, with woolly undercoat. The head and foreside of the legs are short-haired.

25 Hollandse Herdershond (Dutch Shepherd Dog wire-haired)

Appearance identical to that of the short-haired variety, but for the **colour** and the **coat**. The coat is dense, hard, shaggy and standing off from the body, with dense, woolly undercoat.

26 Komondor

Origin and use when the Magyars settled in Hungary in the ninth century having come from Asia by way of the Russian steppes, they brought these dogs with them. The Komondor, a mountain dog, is thought to be related to the Russian Owtcharka. It is used to guard and defend the herd. **Appearance Head** a broad and arched skull with slight stop and rather short, broad and deep muzzle. **Eyes** oval and dark brown. **Ears** U-shaped, hanging low and immobile. **Neck** rather short without throatiness. **Body** fairly short and medium deep with well-rounded ribs. **Legs** not too long and strong in bone. **Feet** large, the hindfeet somewhat larger than the forefeet. **Tail** long. **Coat** unique to this breed and the Puli, it consists of short, dense woolly undercoat which combines with a long, coarse outer-coat to form the characteristic long tassels. It should not be combed as this prevents the felting effect.

24

Height at withers and colour: similar to those of the short-haired.

25

Colour: blue-grey, pepper and salt, gold or silver brindle.

26

Height at withers: dog: average 32 inches (81 cm), at least 26 inches (66 cm), bitch: average 28 inches (71 cm), at least 22 inches (56 cm). Colour: white.

27 Kuvasz

Origin and use like the Komondor and the Puli, this is one of the very old Hungarian breeds. Generally thought to have been brought to Hungary by the Magyars at the same time as the Komondor or perhaps later, about the year 1200, by the Kuman tribes. The Kuvasz is a mountain dog; its duty was to watch and to defend, although in former times it was also used for hunting wolves and wild boar.

Appearance Head a rather long, slightly arched skull, slight stop and broad long muzzle. **Eyes** almond-shaped and dark brown. **Ears** V-shaped drop ears. **Neck** moderately long, without throatiness. **Body** fairly long with long deep chest and slightly arched ribs. **Legs** strong and not too long. **Feet** hind feet longer and narrower than front. **Tail** long. **Coat** is 2–5 inches (4–12 cm) long, with harsh, wavy uppercoat and short, fine, woolly undercoat. The head and the front of the legs are short-haired.

Character courageous, quiet, good watch-dog and guardian, good with children.

28 Lapphund (Lapinkoira, Swedish Lapp Spitz)

Origin and use Lapland, where it was originally used for herding reindeer. Sweden set up a standard for the breed, which was recognized by the Fédération Cynologique Internationale (FCI).

Appearance Head a slightly arched and moderately broad skull, a pronounced stop and medium long wedge-shaped muzzle. **Eyes** large and dark brown, full of expression. **Ears** medium-sized, pointed prick ears. **Neck** moderately long. **Body** rather long with well-sprung ribs. **Legs** strong and not too long. **Feet** oval. **Tail** of slightly less than medium length and curled. **Coat** long, glossy and lying close to the body; the undercoat is dense, woolly and soft. The coat is short on the head and the front of the legs.

Character courageous, intelligent, faithful, good watch-dog, excellent sheep-herding dog, no hunting instinct.

29 Mudi

Origin and use originated in Hungary at the end of the nineteenth or the beginning of the twentieth century. Sheep-herding dog well suited to herding cattle, sheep and geese.

Appearance Head rather narrow, with little stop and a pointed, narrow muzzle. **Eyes** dark brown. **Ears** prick ears. **Neck** strong. **Body** fairly short with sufficiently deep chest and slightly arched ribs. **Legs** moderately long. **Feet** small and short. **Tail** short or docked 2–3 inches (5–7½ cm). **Coat** curly, short on head and feet.

Character lively, energetic, intelligent, untiring, fierce catcher of vermin, good watch-dog.

27
Height at withers:
dog: 28½–30 inches
(72½–76 cm), bitch:
26½–28 inches
(67½–71 cm).
Colour: white.

28
Height at withers:
dog: 18–20 inches
(45½–51 cm), bitch:
16–18 inches
(40½–45½ cm).
Colour: black, bear-
brown, white.

29
Height at withers:
12–20 inches
(30½–51 cm).
Colour: black, white,
white and black or
white and grey, light
to dark grey with
black patches.

30 Norsk Buhund (Norwegian Buhund)

Origin and use Norway. A very old breed which is used for herding cattle, rounding up horses and especially as watch-dogs.
Appearance Head a rather broad and flat skull, marked stop and rather short muzzle. **Eyes** dark brown with an energetic and courageous expression. **Ears** pointed prick ears. **Neck** moderately long without throatiness. **Body** short with a deep chest and well-sprung ribs. **Legs** rather short and strong. **Feet** small and oval. **Tail** tightly curled. **Coat** not too short, thick, coarse, lying close to the body, with soft, woolly undercoat.
Character noisy, attentive, independent, courageous.

Owtcharki (Russian Sheepdog)

Of the numerous types of mountain dogs occurring in European and Asiatic Russia, four were given official recognition in Russia at a Cynological Congress in 1952.

31 Owtcharka (Mid-Asiatic Owtcharka)

Origin as its name indicates, this large, strong and coarse dog occurs in the central lands of Asiatic Russia.
Appearance This varies in some respects according to the areas where the breed occurs. In the north, where the breed was crossed with the Borzoi, it is smaller and less aggressive and the head is somewhat narrower; in the steppes, the frame is lighter and the coat less heavy; in the mountains of Pamir, the breed is larger and stronger, whereas in the territories further east the middle size prevails. **Head** a loose skin and a broad skull, very slight stop and strong, not too large muzzle. **Eyes** deep set, small and round. **Ears** short, triangular drop ears. **Neck** short, with throatiness. **Body** not too long, with deep, broad chest and well-sprung ribs. **Legs** rather long, with strong bone. **Feet** oval. **Coat** 3 inches (7–8 cm) long, hard and straight, with dense and soft undercoat.

32 Owtcharka (Transcaucasian Owtcharka)

Origin and use the shepherds of the Caucasian Mountains needed a dog to herd their flocks which was also large and strong enough to defend them against wolves and thieves. In order to obtain the required dog, sheep-herding Spitz were crossed with Mastiff-type dogs. Nowadays, the best breeding centres are in Georgia and in the neighbourhood of Signach.
Appearance Head a broad skull, very slight stop and rather short, strong muzzle. **Eyes** small and oval. **Ears** small drop ears. **Neck** short and strong. **Body** heavy and rather short with a broad and deep chest. **Legs** rather long with heavy bone. **Feet** large and oval. **Tail** long. **Coat** rather long, dense, coarse and straight, with woolly undercoat. On the head and the front of the legs it is shorter.

33 Owtcharka (North Caucasian Owtcharka)

Origin the steppes and the highlands to the north of the Caucasus and the west of the Caspian Sea.
Appearance Head is somewhat longer and leaner than that of the Transcaucasian Owtcharka. **Body** shorter and lighter. **Legs** longer. **Coat** somewhat shorter.

30

Height at withers:
dog: 18 inches
(45½ cm), bitch:
somewhat less.
Colour: wheaten,
fawn-red, black or
medium dark red.
White markings
allowed.

31

Height at withers:
dog: 25–26 inches
(63½–66 cm), bitch:
24–25 inches
(61–63½ cm).
Colour: black, white,
grey, drab yellow, red,
grey-red, brindle or
speckled.

32

Height at withers
dog: 26 inches
(66 cm), bitch:
25 inches (63½ cm).
Colour: grey, red-grey
or white; one solid
colour or pied.

34 Owtcharka (South Russian Owtcharka)

Origin the breed which nowadays occurs in the Crimea and the south Ukraine originated in the Asturias in northern Spain. They were produced by crossing the Spanish sheep-herding dogs, which accompanied the large flocks of Merino sheep imported into Russia, with Tartar mountain dogs and the Borzoi from the steppes.

Appearance Head a moderately broad skull and a long pointed muzzle. **Ears** medium-sized, triangular drop ears. **Neck** without throatiness. **Body** rather short with moderately broad, deep chest. **Legs** heavy. **Feet** strong. **Tail** long. **Coat** very long and dense.

Character eager to learn and responsive to training.

35 Owczarek Nizinny (Lowlands Shepherd Dog)

Origin Poland, to which it was probably taken by the Huns.

Appearance Head a slightly arched skull which is as long as the muzzle, and marked stop. **Eyes** moderately large, oval and hazel, with a lively expression. **Ears** moderately large drop ears. **Neck** of medium length and without throatiness. **Body** moderately long and has a deep chest with slightly arched ribs. **Legs** lightly boned, not too long and strong. **Feet** oval. **Tail** cropped or the dog is born tailless. **Coat** long, dense and coarse with dense woolly undercoat.

Character lively, intelligent.

36 Owczarek Podhalanski (Tatra Mountain Sheepdog)

Origin and use Poland. The Tibetan Mastiff is believed to be its ancestor. It is a mountain dog used to guard and defend the herd.

Appearance Head a broad, flat skull, marked stop and short muzzle. **Eyes** moderately large, brown, with good expression. **Ears** V-shaped drop ears. **Neck** longish, without throatiness. **Body** rather long with deep and broad chest. **Legs** strongly boned. **Tail** not too long, sometimes missing at birth, or docked. **Coat** rather long, thick, hard, straight or wavy, short on the head and the front of the legs.

Character good-natured, docile, good watch-dog.

34
Height at withers:
20 inches (51 cm).
Colour: white, white
with yellow patches,
ash-grey, grey with
small and large white
spots, white with grey
undercoat which gives
a bluish impression.

35
Height at withers:
dog: 17–20 inches
(43–51 cm), bitch:
16–18½ inches
(40½–47 cm).
Colour: all colours and
markings allowed.

36
Height at withers:
24–34 inches
(61–86½ cm).
Colour: white,
sometimes with
cream markings.

37 Puli

Origin it is believed that, like the Komondor, the Puli came from Asia to Hungary in the ninth century. A true sheepdog, it is not so much the defender as the herder of the cattle and sheep.

Appearance **Head** a round skull, pronounced stop and short muzzle. **Eyes** round, coffee-brown, with a lively and intelligent expression. **Ears** V-shaped drop ears, rounded at the lower end. **Neck** moderately long. **Body** fairly long with moderately broad, deep and long chest. **Legs** strong and not too short. **Feet** short and round. **Tail** long and curled when in movement or roused. **Coat** consists of coarser upperhair and finer woolly underhair. The right proportion of these two determines the required felting.

Character intelligent, happy, devoted, good watch-dog.

38 Pumi

Origin derived from crossing the Puli with breeds of cattle-drovers which came to Hungary in the seventeenth and eighteenth centuries with the flocks of sheep imported from Pomerania and France. The old Pomeranian shepherd's Spitz in particular is considered to be an ancestor of the Pumi. Originally a cattle drover, it is nowadays used to herd cattle and pigs and to destroy rodents and vermin.

Appearance **Head** a rather narrow, arched skull, a hardly noticeable stop and a fairly long snipy muzzle. **Eyes** dark brown. **Ears** mobile tip ears of medium size. **Neck** moderately long. **Body** a short back, a sloping topline and a deep, long chest with rather flat ribs. **Legs** lightly boned and rather long. **Feet** strong. **Tail** curled; short at birth or docked. **Coat** rough, of medium length, it does not felt and has a shaggy appearance.

Character restless, lively, daring, aggressive, yapper, good watchdog.

39 Šar Planina (Yugoslavian Sheepdog)

Origin and use one of the oldest working dogs of Yugoslavia. In former times it was mainly found in Karst and Istria, where it was used in the difficult mountain ranges, but now it is much more widespread.

Appearance **Head** a broad, slightly domed skull, slight stop and broad, deep muzzle. **Eyes** almond-shaped and dark. **Ears** rather long drop ears. **Neck** strong. **Body** of medium length with broad, deep chest and well sprung ribs. **Legs** moderately long. **Feet** round. **Tail** not too long, docking is allowed. **Coat** dense and about 4 inches (10 cm) long, the undercoat is soft; on the head and the front of the legs it is short.

Character intelligent, courageous, trustworthy.

40 Šar Tip (Yugoslavian Sheepdog)

Identical in appearance to the Šar Planina, but for the height at withers, which should exceed 26 inches (65 cm). Is used nowadays for rescue work and as a frontier-guard.

37

Height at withers:
dog: 16–17½ inches
(40½–44½ cm), bitch:
15–16½ inches
(38–41½ cm).
Colour: reddish black
and all shades of grey
and white.

38

Height at withers:
about 14–18 inches
(35½–45½ cm).
Colour: grey or slate,
black and reddish;
white not favoured.

39

Height at withers:
22–24 inches
(56–61 cm).
Colour: iron-grey,
some white on chest
and legs.

41 Schapendoes (Dutch Sheepdog)

Origin the Netherlands. An old breed, akin to the shaggy long-haired sheep-herding dogs of other countries, such as the German Schafpudel, the Puli, the Bearded Collie and the Briard. Still kept as a sheep-herding dog, nowadays it has become more a house dog and watch-dog.

Appearance Head a flat skull which is broader than it is long with marked stop and broad, short muzzle. **Eyes** round, large and brown. **Ears** not too large drop ears. **Neck** not too short. **Body** rather long with a deep chest and slightly arched ribs. **Legs** moderately long and lightly boned. **Feet** large with a broad oval shape. **Tail** long with a hook at the tip. **Coat** long, dense, thin and harsh, slightly wavy and should decidedly not be silky.

Character lively, highly strung, courageous, intelligent, faithful.

42 Sheepdog, Old English (Bobtail)

Origin and use one of the oldest breeds of sheepdogs in England, but its descent is obscure. First used for guarding herds, it later became a cattle drover and sheep-herding dog.

Appearance Head a rather square skull, fairly long and square muzzle and marked stop. **Eyes** dark or wall-eyes. **Ears** small drop ears. **Neck** should be rather long. **Body** short, compact and higher on quarters than at withers, with well-sprung ribs and deep, broad chest. **Legs** moderately long with strong bone. **Feet** small and round. **Tail** entirely docked. **Coat** abundant, long, rough and harsh, with dense undercoat.

Character intelligent, courageous, calm, not pugnacious, good watch-dog and fond of children.

43 Sheepdog, Shetland (Sheltie)

Origin and use the Shetland Isles of Scotland. They probably developed from working Collies from the mainland and the Yakki or Iceland dogs carried by the whaling ships which called at the Shetlands. In comparison with other sheep-herding dogs they are small, but so are the Shetland sheep and ponies. They guard the house, herd the flocks and prevent cattle trampling the fields which are not hedged in on the island.

Appearance Head a flat, moderately broad skull, a slight stop and the muzzle and the skull are of equal length. **Eyes** of medium size, almond-shaped and dark, save for the blue merles, when wall-eyes are allowed. **Ears** small, tip ears. **Neck** rather long. **Body** not short, the chest is deep with well-sprung ribs. **Legs** moderately long with strong bone. **Feet** oval. **Tail** moderately long. **Coat** long, harsh and straight, with a short, dense and soft undercoat.

Character intelligent, gentle, affectionate but not friendly with everybody, good watch-dog.

41

Height at withers:
dog: 17½–20 inches
(44½–51 cm), bitch;
16–18 inches
(40–47 cm).
Colour: all colours
allowed preferably
blue-grey to black.

42

Height at withers:
dog: 22 inches
(56 cm) and higher,
bitch: 20 inches
(51 cm).
Colour: every shade
of grey, grizzle, blue or
blue merle, with or
without white
markings.

43

Height at withers:
dog: 14½ inches
(37 cm), bitch: 14
inches (45½ cm).
Colour: tricolour, from
pale tan, through gold
to dark mahogany or
blue merle; black and
white or black and tan
as further colours.
White markings are
desirable, as a blaze,
a collar, on breast, tip
of tail and on legs.

44 Västgötaspets (Swedish Vallhund)

Origin and use Sweden. Its resemblance to the Pembrokeshire Welsh Corgi is so marked that the breeds are obviously closely related but whether the Västgötaspets reached Sweden in Viking ships or Viking cattle dogs were taken to Britain and became the ancestor of the Corgi has never been proved. Used on the farm for many purposes such as cattle droving, catching vermin and as watch-dogs.

Appearance Head a moderately broad, flat skull, not too pronounced stop and not too long muzzle. **Eyes** round and brown. **Ears** medium sized prick ears. **Neck** rather long. **Body** not too long with well-sprung ribs and deep chest. **Tail** undocked and not longer than 4 inches (10 cm). **Coat** not too short, hard and lies close to the body, undercoat very dense and soft.

Character lively, keen, faithful, good watch-dog.

45 Welsh Corgi (Cardiganshire)

Origin and use very old breed from South Wales, used as drovers and to guard cattle and ponies.

Appearance Head foxy with rather broad, flat skull, slight stop and not too long muzzle. **Eyes** moderately large and dark, except for the blue merle, with a keen and watchful expression. **Ears** rather large prick ears. **Neck** strong and rather long. **Body** fairly long with deep chest and well-sprung ribs. **Legs** short, with strong bone, the front to be slightly bowed. **Feet** rather large and round. **Tail** of medium length. **Coat** harsh and short or medium.

Character calm, intelligent, good with children.

46 Welsh Corgi (Pembrokeshire)

Origin the same as that of the Cardiganshire Corgi.

Appearance Head foxy with rather broad, flat skull, moderate stop and a not too long muzzle. **Eyes** round, of medium size and hazel. **Ears** moderately long prick ears. **Neck** fairly long. **Body** moderately long with well-sprung ribs and a broad, deep chest. **Legs** short, straight and have strong bone. **Feet** oval. **Tail** either docked or the dog is born tailless. **Coat** of moderate length and dense.

Character strong personality, lively, intelligent, bold, affectionate, good with children.

47 Armant (Ermenti, Egyptian Sheepdog)

Origin and use the breed is named after the village of Armant (Ermenti) in Upper Egypt and is supposed to have originated from crossing indigenous dogs with French dogs which came over with the armies of Bonaparte in 1798. At first the Armant was only used as a drover and guard with the herds, but now it often serves as a watch-dog, because it is very aggressive to strangers.

Appearance Head narrow and not too long, with a pronounced stop and a long, somewhat pointed muzzle. **Eyes** brown. **Ears** small drop or prick ears. **Tail** long, sometimes docked. **Coat** long, rough and shaggy. There is a noticeable moustache. **Height at withers** 22 inches (56 cm). **Colour** All shades of grey, greyish yellow. The mask should be dark, the topknot, muzzle and breast should always be white.

44

Height at withers:
13–16 inches
(33–40½ cm).
Colour: grey with dark
tips, red-yellow, grey-
brown, brown-yellow,
brindle or blue and
grey pied; a few white
markings are allowed.

45

Height at withers:
about 12 inches
(30½ cm).
Colour: all colours
except pure white.

46

Height at withers:
10–12 inches
(25½–30½ cm).
Colour: solid red,
reddish brown, sable,
fawn or black and tan.
White markings on
legs, neck and breast
allowed.

48 Australian Cattle Dog (Heeler)

Origin and use originated from the Kelpie, a blue merle Collie and supposedly the Dalmatian. It drives unwilling cattle by snapping at their heels. The breed is becoming more popular with the general public.
Appearance Head a strong sheep-herding dog's head with tip ears. **Chest** of medium length, broad and deep. **Tail** long. **Coat** short and rather hard, with dense undercoat. **Height at withers** dog: 18–20 inches (45½–51 cm), bitch: 17–19 inches (43–48½ cm). **Colour** blue or red speckled with tan, blue or black.

49 Barb

Identical to the Kelpie, but always black and the height about 24 inches (61 cm).

50 Berger du Languedoc (Farou)

Origin the south of France.
Appearance Head rather long, with little stop and pointed muzzle. **Eyes** large, dark yellow and with a lively expression. **Ears** cropped. **Body** a deep chest which is not too strongly boned. **Legs** must have a dew claw (sometimes there are two). **Feet** rather long. **Tail** usually docked. **Coat** in most cases short but sometimes long or half long, although always short on the head. **Height at withers**: dog: 16–20 inches (40½–51 cm), bitch: 15–20 inches (38–51 cm). **Colour** black with yellow markings, reddish or reddish and black.

51 Hrvatski Ovcar (Croatian Sheepdog)

Origin and use an old indigenous Yugoslavian breed in Slavonia and the surrounding country used for herding and as a watch-dog.
Appearance Head rather long with a moderately broad skull and not too long muzzle, which is neither pointed nor blunt. **Eyes** almond-shaped and dark. **Ears** moderately large, triangular prick or tip ears. **Neck** medium-sized, not too heavy and without throatiness. **Body** moderately long and slender with broad and not too deep chest and slightly-sprung ribs. **Legs** not too long. **Feet** cat-feet. **Tail** long and bushy, carried high when working, but may be docked short. Some dogs are born tailless. **Coat** 3–6 inches (7½–15 cm) long, soft, wavy or curly, short on the head. **Height at withers** light type: 15–17½ inches (38–44 cm), heavy type: up to 20 inches (51 cm). **Colour** black, sometimes speckled with grey-white.
Character courageous, lively, good watch-dog.

52 Hütespitz

Origin and use Germany, where it is used exclusively for work with cattle.
Appearance Head long with a round skull, no stop and a deep, not too short muzzle. **Eyes** dark brown. **Ears** prick ears. **Neck** short and strong. **Body** rather short, with broad back and long, deep chest. **Legs** rather long. **Feet** long. **Tail** long. **Coat** rather long and hard, with dense, woolly undercoat. **Height at withers** dog: 20–24 inches (51–61 cm), bitch: 20–23 inches (51–58½ cm). **Colour** white, sometimes with yellowish markings.
Character intelligent, gentle, affectionate, tolerant, good watch-dog.

53 Kelpie

Origin most probably originated by crossing the Dingo (the indigenous wild dog) and the Scotch and working Collies.

Appearance Head a typical shepherd dog's head with prick ears. **Feet** cat-feet. **Tail** long. **Coat** short and smooth. **Height at withers** dog: 18–20 inches (45½–51 cm), bitch: 17–19 inches (43–48½ cm). **Colour** black, blue, black and tan, red, red and tan or fawn chocolate.

54 Labrit

Origin a dog of the Landes, in the south-west of France which is akin to the Pyrenean Sheepdogs and in the main resembles them.

Appearance Coat long, dull and dry (like goat's hair). **Height at withers** 19–22 inches (48½–56 cm). **Colour** light or dark drab red, possibly with some black hairs.

55 Lapin Porokoira (Laponian Vallhund)

Origin and use developed in south Finland as a dog with great stamina, able to guard the reindeer herds, by crossing the Lapphund with the German Shepherd Dog and the Collie.

Appearance Head moderately long and broad. **Eyes** brown. **Ears** prick ears. **Neck** fairly long. **Body** rather long with well-sprung ribs and deep chest. **Legs** medium length and strong. **Feet** oval. **Tail** long. **Coat** dense and long, with abundant undercoat. **Height at withers** dog: 20–22 inches (51–56 cm), bitch: 17–20 inches (43–51 cm). **Colour** black or black and tan, the tan often mingled with grey.

Character strong, little hunting instinct.

56 Pommerscher Hütehund (Pomeranian Sheepdog)

Origin and use Germany, where it is kept exclusively for work with the flocks.

Appearance Head long, with a narrow skull, slight stop and a strong, fine muzzle. **Eyes** dark brown. **Ears** small drop ears. **Neck** moderate length. **Body** a deep chest. **Legs** rather long. **Feet** oval. **Tail** long. **Coat** of medium length, soft, with dense, woolly undercoat. **Height at withers** dog: 20–24 inches (51–61 cm), bitch: 20–22 inches (51–56 cm). **Colour** white with or without yellowish markings.

Character the same as that of the Hütespitz.

57 Rumanian Sheepdog

Origin old indigenous Rumanian breed.

Appearance Head a broad and flat skull and a not too short, rather deep muzzle. **Eyes** oval. **Ears** small, triangular drop ears. **Neck** short and heavy. **Body** rather long, with broad back and deep chest. **Legs** rather long and heavy. **Feet** oval. **Tail** of medium length. **Coat** moderately long and lank, with abundant undercoat. **Height at withers** about 24 inches (61 cm). **Colour** red- or brown-pied, sandy, greyish or brown.

Character sharp, distrustful with strangers, good watch-dog.

Guard and utility dogs

In this group breeds of very different descent have been brought together. Nevertheless, these breeds all carry a hereditary aptitude to guard and to defend, characteristics which were already predominant long ago, due to man's selection of their forebears. The largest dogs in the group are the mastiffs, which in ancient times accompanied armies and took an active part in battle as useful auxiliaries. The Roman fighting-dogs, Molossian Hounds, were also mastiffs and they were used to fight large beasts of prey for sport or were set against their own kind in the arena. Long after the ways of warfare had altered and animal fights had been forbidden by law, several breeds of calm, self-confident house dogs developed from these original types and with most of them there is no longer any danger of savageness.

Through the ages, mastiffs have been devoted to their owners and ready to defend their master, his kin and his belongings to the utmost. This quality has always been preserved and makes these breeds especially fit as watch-dogs on country estates. In outward appearance all the mastiffs have in common a large, short and broad head, drop ears and very heavy bones. Their powerful build gives all these breeds an impressive appearance which in itself can prevent the approach of intruders where they are guardians of house and farmyard. This is equally true of the English Bulldog, although it is not a very large dog. Mastiffs are not the best choice as house dogs in small houses or apartments, for which the other breeds included in the group are much more suitable.

Although, at first sight, the spitz and pole dogs resemble each other closely, and no demarcation-line has ever been drawn between them, it is wrong to suppose that they are of the same descent. Both the spitz and the pole dogs (which probably carry more wolf blood) have always been used as 'jacks-of-all-trades'. Hard-working dogs, they have been (and most pole dogs still are) used as watch-dogs, guardians of the herds, for hunting, as pack-dogs and for drawing sleighs. Moreover, in the tents of the nomadic tribes, children would curl up against their thick coats to keep warm at night. The forebears of the modern breeds in this group already lived in close contact with human families. Their present representatives are also very clean and adaptable animals. They are good companions and take a lively interest in all that happens in and around the house.

The spitz are very watchful and bark at the slightest real or supposed alarm, which will at once deter any prospective burglars. In their own way, their behaviour is as preventive as that of the mastiffs, and, like them, spitz are ready and fit to take action if necessary. They are not otherwise pugnacious, but are reserved with strangers.

The representatives of a third category belonging to this group, the pinschers and the schnauzers, sometimes called 'the terriers of Germany', are descended from old German village dogs crossed with many other breeds to produce these flat- and rough-coated dogs respectively. They bark less but are more intelligent than the spitz. A consistent and stern training is necessary in order to develop the good qualities of their strong character. If this is not tackled in the right way, they will get the upper hand and become unmanageable. Although by nature they are not inclined to be friendly to other dogs, this will not raise many difficulties, provided they are kept under good control.

Scale of Guard and Utility Dog illustrations 1 :15

58 Ainu (Hokkaido Ken)

Origin One of the oldest Japanese breeds, bred for hunting and as a watch-dog by the Ainu, the original inhabitants of the island of Hokkaido.
Appearance Head moderately broad skull, rather short muzzle ending in a blunt point and slight stop. **Eyes** narrow and dark. **Ears** prick ears. **Neck** of medium length and strong. **Body** not too short with deep chest and well sprung ribs. **Legs** moderately long and strong. **Feet** oval. **Tail** curled. **Coat** thick, rather short and straight, with thick undercoat.
Character courageous, obedient, intelligent, energetic.

59 Akita Inu

Origin this ancient breed, of Polar origin, is the largest and best known of the Japanese breeds. Similar dogs are portrayed on reliefs dating back to 2000 BC and the history of the breed has been recorded for over 300 years. They take their name from the province of Akita and they were used for hunting boar and deer. Now they are much appreciated as watch-dogs and army dogs.
Appearance Head fairly broad skull, medium long and strong muzzle, slight stop. **Eyes** small, deep set and dark brown. **Ears** small, triangular prick ears, **Neck** not too long and strong. **Body** not too short with deep and rather broad chest and slightly arched ribs. **Legs** of moderate length and well boned. **Feet** short. **Tail** moderately long and carried in a slight curve or curled over the back. **Coat** of medium length, hard, straight and standing off from the body, with dense, soft and woolly undercoat.
Character trustworthy, active, good watch-dog.

60 Alaskan Malamute

Origin this indigenous sleigh-dog from Alaska is named after an Eskimo tribe. Long used by merchants and missionaries in Alaska for all work in those regions, the breed first appeared at a show outside its native country in 1926.
Appearance Head skull which is wide between the ears and narrow towards the muzzle, which in its turn narrows slightly towards the point of the nose. **Eyes** almond-shaped and dark. **Ears** medium sized triangular prick ears. **Neck** moderately long and strong. **Body** short, with deep chest and well-sprung ribs. **Legs** of medium size, strong, with heavy bone. **Feet** large and strong. **Tail** long, not too stiffly curled and carried gaily. **Coat** not long but thick, dense and coarse, with a dense, oily, woolly undercoat.
Character affectionate, kind, intelligent, obedient, good with children, responsive to training.

58
Height at withers:
two sizes. About 16½
inches (40½ cm) or
about 20 inches
(51 cm).
Colour: red, white,
black, pepper and salt,
black with brown
markings.

59
Height at withers:
20–27 inches
(50–68½ cm).
Colour: fawn,
wheaten, grey, white,
brindle, black, black
and tan.

60
Height at withers:
dog: 22–25 inches
(56–63 cm), bitch:
20–23 inches
(50–58 cm).
Colour: wolf-grey or
from light grey through
to black with white
mask and underparts.

61 Boxer

Origin in Bavaria, where the first Boxers to be registered in the studbook were bred from the descendants of the large and heavy Danziger Bullenbeiszer, the small Brabanter Bullenbeiszer and the English Bulldog.
Appearance Head slightly arched skull with distinct stop. The powerful muzzle is short, broad, and deep, and curves slightly upwards. **Eyes** moderately round, large and dark. **Ears** set high on the head and still cropped in some countries, including the United States and Germany. **Neck** long, dry and strongly muscled. **Body** deep chest, well-sprung ribs, short and broad straight back. **Legs** moderately long with large bones. **Feet** cat-feet. **Tail** docked moderately short. **Coat** short and hard.
Character lively, pugnacious, affectionate, kind with children.

62 Bulldog

Origin fights between dogs and bulls were held in England as long ago as the thirteenth century. This sport, later called bull-baiting, became so popular that dogs were specially bred for it. Bull-baiting was prohibited by law in most countries in the middle of the nineteenth century. The breed has been kept pure for the last 200 years, although at short periods in the last century crossings with Pugs, Spanish dogs and English Mastiffs are said to have taken place to achieve particular improvements.
Appearance Head huge, deep, with broad square skull, very short broad muzzle with upturned lower jaw and heavy folds between the nose and the deep stop. **Eyes** round and very dark. **Ears** small, thin rose ears. **Neck** rather short, heavy, with much throatiness. **Body** short, broad in front and narrow behind, with very deep, broad and round chest, markedly arched ribs and roach back. **Forelegs** rather short, very strongly boned and placed far apart. **Hindlegs** longer than the forelegs. **Feet** almost round. **Tail** hanging, rather short, thick at the root and tapering quickly to a fine point. **Coat** fine, short, dense and soft.
Character courageous, good-natured, very affectionate and loyal to all close friends, man and beast, not pugnacious.

63 Bull Mastiff

Origin the breed originated in England by crossing the Bulldog with the Mastiff. Although not officially recognized until 1924, a similar dog had existed for a century and was often used by gamekeepers on their night patrols.
Appearance Head large, square skull; short, broad and deep muzzle; marked stop. **Eyes** dark or hazel. **Ears** V-shaped drop ears. **Neck** moderately long and heavy. **Body** short with broad, deep chest and well sprung ribs. **Legs** of moderate length and strongly boned. **Feet** not too large cat-feet. **Tail** long. **Coat** short and hard.
Character happy, trustworthy, attentive, affectionate, good with children, good watch-dog.

61

Height at withers:
dog: about 22–24
inches (56–60 cm),
bitch: about 21–23
inches (53½–58½ cm).
Colour: yellow or
brindle, with or
without white. The
white should be
limited to a third of the
ground colour.
Dark mask and
dark-rimmed eyes.

62

Weight: dog: 55 lb
(almost 25 kg), bitch:
50 lb (22½ kg).
Colour: of little
consequence, but
never black, black and
white or black and tan.

63

Height at withers:
dog: 25–27 inches
(63½–68½ cm), bitch:
24–26 inches
(61–66 cm).
Colour: every shade of
brindle, fawn, red.
Muzzle, ears and nose
should be black.

64 Canaan Dog

Origin the national breed of Israel, it was bred out of Pariah dogs, the half-wild dogs which are common in parts of North Africa and the countries of the Near East. According to *The World Encyclopedia of Dogs* there are two types—Collie and Dingo—which differ in appearance. The aim was to obtain a dog fit for diverse purposes which could withstand the climate and indigenous diseases better than imported breeds.

Appearance Head fairly wide skull, not too long and moderately broad muzzle with little stop. **Eyes** dark. **Ears** short, broad prick ears; tip, drop and pendant ears are permissible. **Neck** of medium length. **Body** short, with deep, not too narrow chest. **Legs** rather long. **Feet** round. **Tail** curled over the back. **Coat** of medium length, straight and hard; long hair is permissible but not desirable. **Legs** should be well feathered and the tail plumed.

Character intelligent, responsive to training, good watch-dog.

65 Cão da Serra da Estrêla (Portuguese Mountain Dog)

Origin mountain dog from the Portuguese Serra da Estrêla, known for many centuries.

Appearance Head large with broad, moderately long skull, strong muzzle (which is as long as the skull) and little stop. **Eyes** oval and dark amber. **Ears** small triangular drop ears; in Portugal cropping is allowed. **Neck** short and heavy with little throatiness. **Body** should not be too short, with deep, broad chest and lightly arched ribs. **Legs** rather long with strong bones. **Feet** round rather than long. **Tail** long. **Coat** like goat's hair, coarse, harsh, moderately long, flat or slightly wavy; or may be a long-haired dense uppercoat with woolly, soft undercoat.

Character trustworthy watch-dog.

66 Cão d'Água (Portuguese Water Dog)

Origin nothing is clear about the origin of this water dog which was formerly used as a hunting dog and is now the much appreciated assistant of the fishermen along the whole coast of Portugal. It is helpful in salvaging drifting tackle and guards the fishing boats on the shore.

Appearance Head long, not too broad skull, robust muzzle which is somewhat shorter than the skull and marked stop. **Eyes** round and varying in colour from black to brown. **Ears** heart-shaped drop ears. **Neck** short, round and strong. **Body** short, with a deep, broad chest and well-sprung ribs. **Legs** rather long and well-boned. **Feet** round, somewhat flat, and webbed to the tip of the toes. **Tail** long and carried strongly curled. **Coat** there are two varieties; long, slightly wavy, not too dense, glossy, with a good topknot on the head or a shorter curl coat which is very dense and dull. There is no undercoat.

Character pugnacious, energetic, obedient, one-man dog.

64

Height at withers:
20–24 inches
(51–61 cm).
Colour: sandy to tan,
white or black. Large
white markings are
preferred on all colours
and harlequin patterns
and white and black
marks are permitted.

65

Height at withers:
dog: 27–28 inches
(68½–71 cm), bitch:
25–27 inches
(63½–68½ cm).
Colour: fawn with
black mask, grey
patched white and all
other colours. Solid
white or black seldom
occur.

66

Height at withers:
dog: 20–23 inches
(51–58½ cm), bitch:
17–21 inches
(43–53½ cm).
Colour: black or black
and white, brown or
brown and white,
light grey, dark grey or
solid white.

67 Cão de Castro Laboreiro (Portuguese Watchdog)

Origin a guard dog rather than a herder, but one of Portugal's two major sheepdogs (the other is the Serra de Aires), which occurs in the mountains of the Peneda and Suajo, between the rivers Minho and Lima. It has proved to be very responsive to training as a police dog.

Appearance Head rather long with moderately wide skull, slight stop and a long, strong, slightly-pointed muzzle. **Eyes** almond-shaped and dark. **Ears** pendant. **Neck** fairly short and broad. **Body** not too short, with deep chest and well-sprung ribs. **Legs** rather long and heavily-boned. **Feet** oval. **Tail** long. **Coat** rather short, hard and dense.

Character affectionate, bold, good watch-dog.

68 Cão Rafeiro do Alentejo (Portuguese Shepherd Dog)

Origin the Alentejo province of Portugal, south of Lisbon. An imposing mastiff-like dog, used for guarding the herds.

Appearance Head bear-like, with wide skull; the muzzle is shorter than the skull, not too broad, with little stop. **Eyes** small and dark. **Ears** small, triangular drop ears. **Neck** strong, short, with throatiness. **Body** fairly long and has a broad, deep chest with slightly-arched ribs. **Legs** rather long with strong bones. **Feet** short and strong. **Tail** long. **Coat** short or half-long, coarse, smooth and dense.

Character self-confident, watchful especially at night, aggressive.

69 Chien des Pyrénées (Pyrenean Mountain Dog)

Origin this is another dog which, together with the Spanish Mastins and the Italian Mastino, is descended from the very ancient Tibetan Mastiff. The breed was very much in fashion during the seventeenth century, but was quite forgotten until recent years. It is now the most popular of these three very old breeds, even outside its native country. It was originally used to guard the flocks against wolves and bears in the mountains of the Ariège.

Appearance Head broad, slightly arched skull, fairly long, broad muzzle and slight stop. **Eyes** rather small, amber coloured, with an intelligent, musing expression. **Ears** small, triangular drop ears. **Neck** fairly short, with little throatiness. **Body** long, the chest broad and deep with slightly-arched ribs. **Legs** rather long, heavily-boned, with one single claw on hing legs. **Feet** not too long. **Tail** long. **Coat** dense, rather long and soft.

Character not pugnacious, diligent, intelligent, good with children.

67

Height at withers:
dog: 22–24 inches
(56–61 cm), bitch:
21–23 inches
(53½–58½ cm).
Colour: all shades of
grey with or without
black mask, dark fawn
and brindle.

68

Height at withers:
dog: 26–29 inches
(66–73½ cm), bitch:
25–27½ inches
(63½–69 cm).
Colour: black, wolf-
grey, deer-brown,
yellow; white
markings or white,
marked with these
colours.

69

Height at withers:
dog: 28–32 inches
(71–81 cm), bitch:
26–29 inches
(66–73½ cm).
Colour: white or white
with preferably
badger, grey, pale
yellow or wolf-grey
patches on the head,
the ears and the root
of the tail.

70 Deutsche Dogge (Great Dane)

Origin dogs of the Great Dane type were carved on Egyptian monuments 5100 years ago, and in many countries similar light Mastiffs occurred which were used for hunting. They were often called Danish Dogs, a name which probably came from the times of the Norsemen, who were keen sportsmen. In Germany, these light Mastiffs were crossed with Greyhounds and the offspring was given the name of Deutsche Dogge (German Mastiff). Outside Germany the breed is often called Great Dane.

Appearance Head long, rather narrow skull, marked stop and long, broad muzzle. **Eyes** of medium size, round and dark, with a lively, intelligent expression. **Ears** drop ears, in Germany they must be cropped. **Neck** long and strong without throatiness. **Body** short with broad, deep chest and well-sprung ribs. **Legs** round. **Tail** long. **Coat** short and glossy.

Character friendly (though not with everyone), affectionate, intelligent and lively.

71 Dobermann Pinscher

Origin bred as guard dogs by Louis Dobermann, of Apolda in Germany, between 1865 and 1890 from very vicious Pinschers. Later, Otto Göller improved the breed, which carries very mixed blood: German blood from the Pinscher, the Thüringian Shepherd Dog, the German Pointer, the Rottweiler and English blood from the Greyhound and the Manchester Terrier. After the turn of the century no more foreign blood was added.

Appearance Head fairly narrow, flat skull, rather long and deep muzzle and slight stop. **Eyes** round, of medium size, dark brown, with an intelligent and energetic expression. **Ears** drop ears or cropped. **Neck** long and dry. **Body** short with moderately broad and deep chest and slightly-arched ribs. **Legs** rather long with strong bones. **Feet** short. **Tail** docked. **Coat** short, dense and hard.

Character faithful, undaunted, courageous, vicious with strangers, intelligent, alert watch-dog, responsive to training.

72 Dogue de Bordeaux

Origin a very old French breed that is supposed to be descended directly from the ancient Roman Molossus and the Mastiffs of Tibet. They became the butchers' dogs of Bordeaux and environs and were used in the South of France to fight bears, wolves and wild donkeys. At the end of the nineteenth century they were crossed with Mastiffs in order to obtain fresh blood and more height at withers.

Appearance Head enormously large and heavy, the circumference of the skull is equal to or surpasses the height at withers, the muzzle is short and square with light folds of skin, the mouth is at least half an inch undershot; distinct stop. **Eyes** oval and large. **Ears** small drop ears, in France cropping is allowed. **Neck** enormously thick and strong. **Body** heavy, moderately long, with very deep, broad chest and well-sprung ribs. **Legs** fairly short with very heavy bone. **Feet** large and short. **Tail** long. **Coat** fine, short and silky.

Character calm, affectionate, good with children, excellent watch-dog.

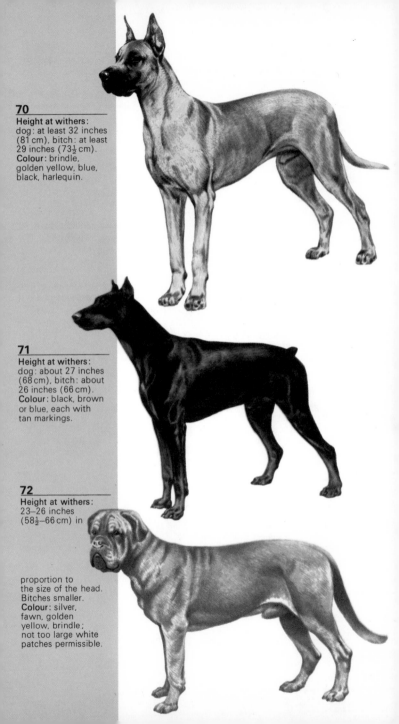

70

Height at withers:
dog: at least 32 inches
(81 cm), bitch: at least
29 inches (73½ cm).
Colour: brindle,
golden yellow, blue,
black, harlequin.

71

Height at withers:
dog: about 27 inches
(68 cm), bitch: about
26 inches (66 cm).
Colour: black, brown
or blue, each with
tan markings.

72

Height at withers:
23–26 inches
(58½–66 cm) in

proportion to
the size of the head.
Bitches smaller.
Colour: silver,
fawn, golden
yellow, brindle;
not too large white
patches permissible.

73 Husky (Eskimo Dog)

Origin probably originating from east Siberia, various types of these sleigh-dogs occur in Greenland, Labrador, Alaska and northern Canada. The Husky has been recognized by the FCI as a Canadian breed.

Appearance Head wedge-shaped, with broad skull, strong muzzle of medium length and little stop. **Eyes** small and deep set. **Ears** short prick ears. **Neck** short, heavy and strong. **Body** not too short, with deep and broad chest and well-sprung ribs. **Legs** rather long, strongly-boned. **Feet** large. **Tail** long, carried gaily or curled over the back. **Coat** the outer-coat 3–6 inches (8–15 cm) long or even longer in some strains, with thick, woolly undercoat.

Character distrustful of strangers, good watch-dog.

74 Fila Brasileiro (Onceiro)

Origin when the Spaniards and Portuguese embarked on the conquest of Central America they took their mastiff-type hunting and fighting dogs into battle. In Brazil, especially, the crossing of these dogs with indigenous dogs developed the Fila Brasileiro. On large estates they are used as watch-dogs and cattle drovers and as sleuth hounds for hunting big game.

Appearance Head large and heavy with broad skull, short broad muzzle and little stop. **Eyes** deep-set, almond-shaped and dark. **Ears** large drop or rose ears. **Neck** not long, strong, with throatiness. **Body** moderately long with broad and deep chest and well-sprung ribs; higher at quarters than at withers. **Legs** long with heavy bone. **Feet** short and strong. **Tail** long. **Coat** short, soft and dense.

Character courageous, friendly, gentle and obedient to its master, unfriendly to strangers.

75 Hovawarth

Origin dogs named Hofewart (meaning estate dog or farmyard 'warden'), are mentioned and reproduced in documents and pictures of about 1473. German breeders recreated this dog out of peasants' dogs from the Harz, the Black Forest and other low mountain districts. The breed was recognized in 1936 under the name Hovawarth.

Appearance Head rather long with broad skull which is as long as the strong and not too pointed muzzle, slight stop. **Eyes** almond-shaped, preferably dark. **Ears** triangular drop ears. **Neck** of medium length without throatiness. **Body** moderately long with a broad, deep chest. **Legs** of medium length and strongly-boned. **Feet** of medium size. **Tail** long. **Coat** long, except on the head and the foreside of the legs where it is short.

Character intelligent, trustworthy, responsive to training, good watch-dog.

73

Height at withers:
dog: 23–26 inches
(58½–66 cm), bitch:
20–23 inches
(51–58½ cm).
Colour: unimportant.
Of frequent occur-
rence are grey, white,
black, black and white
with tan markings
above the eyes.

74

Height at withers:
27 inches (68½ cm).
Colour: All solid
colours or brindle are
permissible, except
white which should be
confined to the feet
and tip of the tail.

75

Height at withers:
dog: 24–28 inches
(61–71 cm), bitch:
22–26 inches
(56–66 cm).
Colour: black, black
and gold, or deep gold.

76 Karabash

Origin this Turkish sheepdog is a descendant of the mastiffs which existed 3,000 years ago in the Middle East. They are the watch-dogs of the American shepherds, but many good specimens are also to be found in the Provinces of Konya and Sivas. The first representatives of the breed in England arrived in 1965.

Appearance Head a broad skull and short, strong muzzle. **Eyes** golden brown. **Ears** V-shaped drop ears which in Turkey are cropped. **Body** rather long with a broad, deep chest. **Legs** fairly long, the hindquarters lighter than the forequarters. **Tail** long. **Coat** short and dense.

Character intrepid, faithful, attentive, good watch-dog.

77 Landseer (European type)

Origin it was long a matter of controversy whether or not the self-coloured and the black and white Newfoundland belonged to the same breed. In England the question was settled in 1886 in favour of one single breed, but on the Continent the contention lasted longer, until 1960 when the FCI recognized the Landseer European type as a separate breed.

Appearance Head broad skull; marked stop and muzzle which is as long as it is deep. **Eyes** almond-shaped, rather deep set, brown to dark brown, with a friendly expression. **Ears** triangular drop ears. **Neck** heavy and strong without pronounced throatiness. **Body** not too short, with deep and broad chest, well-sprung ribs. **Legs** of medium length, strongly-boned. **Feet** large cat-feet. **Tail** long. **Coat** long, dense and straight with soft undercoat shorter on the head and foreside of the legs.

Character affectionate, intelligent, good watch-dog.

78 Leonberger (Leonberg Dog)

Origin named after Leonberg in Würtemberg, Germany, where the breed was created in about 1860 by crossing the Landseer Newfoundland, the Saint Bernard and the Pyrenean Mountain Dog. The breed was not developed to achieve any specific aim.

Appearance Head tolerably wide skull; broad, not too short muzzle; slight stop. **Eyes** light brown to brown with an intelligent, good-natured expression. **Ears** drop ears. **Neck** moderately long, without much throatiness. **Body** of medium length, with deep chest and ribs which are not too round. **Legs** long, strongly-boned. **Feet** almost round. **Tail** long. **Coat** fairly soft to hard, lies close to the body and is rather short except on the head and the front of the legs where it is short.

Character faithful, intelligent, eager to learn, good watch-dog.

76

Height at withers:
dog: 26–30 inches
(66–76 cm), bitch:
somewhat less.
Colour: cream to fawn
or brindle with black
mask and ears.

77

**Height at
withers:** dog:
average 29--32
inches (73½–
81 cm), bitch:
27–29 inches
(68½–73½ cm).
Colour: white with
black head, white
blaze and black
patches on body and
loins. The neck, breast,
belly, legs and tail
should be white.
Black ticks in the
white are
undesirable.

78

Height at withers:
dog: at least 30 inches
(76 cm), bitch: at least
27 inches (68 cm).
Colour: light yellow,
golden to reddish
brown; preferably with
black mask.

79 Mastiff

Origin the oldest English breed and one of the oldest in the world.
Appearance Head wide, square skull; broad, deep, short muzzle; marked stop. **Eyes** small, dark hazel. **Ears** small, thin drop ears. **Neck** fairly long and heavy. **Body** long with broad, deep chest and well-arched ribs. **Legs** long and strongly-boned. **Feet** large and round. **Tail** long **Coat** short.
Character good-natured, courageous, docile, intelligent, good with children.

80 Mastin de los Pirineos (Pyrenean Mastiff)

Origin this Spanish dog is a close kin to the French Pyrenean Mountain Dog with which it probably formed one single breed which has gradually developed into several types.
Appearance Head large, with wide skull, short, broad muzzle, marked stop. **Eyes** small and dark, with slight haw. **Ears** small drop ears, sometimes cropped. **Neck** heavy with throatiness. **Body** broad, deep chest. **Legs** rather long with plenty of bone and double dew claws. **Feet** strong. **Tail** long, sometimes docked. **Coat** moderately long, thick and shaggy.
Character intelligent, good watch-dog.

81 Mastin Español (Mastin Extremeno, Mastin Manchego, Spanish Mastiff)

Origin Spain. Descended from the heavy medieval mastiffs and originally a watch-dog, it proved to be suited to hunting larger game and is nowadays also trained for military purposes.
Appearance Head a wide skull, not too short muzzle, marked stop. **Eyes** small with a haw. **Ears** small drop ears and often cropped, although this is now discouraged. **Neck** heavy with two equally large dew laps. **Body** fairly long with broad, deep chest and well-sprung ribs. **Legs** of medium length, strongly-boned. **Feet** strong. **Tail** long. **Coat** dense, not too short.
Character courageous, responsive to training.

79

Height at withers:
dog: about 30 inches
(76 cm), bitch: about
27½ inches (69 cm).
Colour: apricot, silver
fawn, fawn, brindle.
Black mask.

80

Height at withers:
dog: 28–32 inches
(71–81 cm), bitch:
26–29 inches
(66–73½ cm).
Colour: white or white
with badger-coloured,
drab-yellow or wolf-
grey patches on the
head; a few patches
on the body allowed.

81

Height at withers:
dog: 26–28 inches
(66–71 cm), bitch:
somewhat less.
Colour: black and
white and golden,
reddish, flecked, solid
white, white with
black patches.

82 Mastino Napolitano (Neapolitan Mastiff)

Origin southern Italy. Descended from the old Roman Molossus. The breed rarely occurs abroad.

Appearance Head large, heavy with wide skull, short, square muzzle, marked stop. Eyes fairly large, chestnut brown, with a lively expression. Ears short, triangular tip ears, often cropped. Neck of medium length and massive, with much loose skin and throatiness. Body rather short, with deep, round chest. Legs rather long, strongly-boned. Feet compact. Tail long. Coat short and glossy.

Character faithful, affectionate, energetic, calm, obedient, good watch-dog, attacks only on command.

83 Newfoundland

Origin is is supposed that the breed developed from dogs, possibly Pyrenean Mountain Dogs, which seamen brought to Newfoundland. Certainly,. by 1732 there were large, bear-like dogs on the island, which helped the fishermen by dragging nets and drawing carts and sleighs. It is a genuine water dog; its oily undercoat keeps water well away from the skin and there are many occasions where Newfoundlands have saved men from drowning.

Appearance Head broad and heavy, with short, rather square muzzle, marked, but not sharp stop. Eyes small, rather deep set, dark brown. Ears small drop ears. Neck strong, not too long. Body not too short, with deep, broad chest and well-sprung ribs. Legs of moderate length, strongly-boned. Feet large and strong. Tail of moderate length. Coat double, long and coarse, greasy to the touch, lying close to the body.

Character calm, trustworthy, self-confident, gentle, courageous.

84 Newfoundland, Landseer

Appearance the same as that of the Newfoundland, except for the **colour**, which is white with black patches which should preferably be symmetrical.

85 Norrbottenspets

Origin the Spitz of northern Sweden (Norrbotten). Although practically extinct in 1948, enough representatives of the breed were extant about 1960 to have it recognized and it is now popular in its native country.

Appearance Head moderately broad skull, rather short, pointed muzzle with slight stop. Eyes dark. Ears large prick ears. Neck of medium length. Body rather short, with deep chest, well sprung ribs. Legs medium length. Feet oval. Tail long and curled. Coat dense and hard, with soft, woolly undercoat.

Character lively, happy, good watch-dog.

82

Height at withers:
dog: 26–30 inches
(66–76 cm), bitch:
24–28 inches
(61–71 cm).
Colour: black, lead-
grey, brindle, dapple;
white markings on
breasts and toes occur.

83

Height at withers:
dog: 28½ inches
(71 cm), bitch: 26½
inches (66 cm).
Colour: black, bronze.
Small white or bronze
markings on chest and
toes permissible.
'Landseers' are white
and black (see
separate entry).

85

Height at withers:
should not exceed
15¾ inches (39 cm).
Colour: white with
black, cream or red
markings.

86 Oesterreichischer Kurzhaar Pinscher (Austrian Pinscher)

Origin an old indigenous Austrian breed which is not seen at shows outside its native country.

Appearance Head wide skull, strong and long muzzle, marked stop. **Eyes** round and dark. **Ears** preferably button ears but hanging, prick and rose ears round dark. **Ears** preferably button ears but hanging, prick and rose ears are also allowed. **Neck** strong and rather short. **Body** short with a deep and broad chest, tough ribs. **Legs** of moderate length, heavily-boned. **Feet** short and strong. **Tail** short, heavy and curled, docking is allowed. **Coat** rather short or short, with undercoat.

Character courageous, lively, good watch-dog.

87 Pinscher

Origin the Pinscher is one of the oldest indigenous German breeds, the origins of which have never been determined. In 1890 the Pinschers were still a medley of types, colours, coats and sizes. The short- and rough-haired varieties (the latter being the Schnauzers) are now recognized breeds.

Appearance Head moderately wide skull, not too long muzzle, slight stop. **Eyes** round and dark, with an intelligent and lively expression. **Ears** drop ears, in Germany they are always cropped. **Neck** moderately long and slender, without throatiness. **Body** short with a deep chest. **Legs** of medium length and well-boned. **Feet** small and round. **Tail** docked rather short. **Coat** short, dense and glossy.

Character happy, active, attentive, trustworthy, suspicious of strangers—making a good watch-dog, excellent ratter.

88 Riesenschnauzer (Giant Schnauzer)

Origin originally drovers and guard dogs bred by peasants and cattle dealers in the Bavarian highlands from local cattle and sheep-herding dogs, possibly crossed with Great Danes and Bouviers des Flandres.

Appearance Head long, not too broad skull, long, strong muzzle, moderate stop. **Eyes** oval and dark. **Ears** cropped where this is permitted and dogs may be shown cropped or uncropped in the United States. **Neck** fairly long, without throatiness. **Body** short, with a very deep and broad chest, slightly-arched ribs. **Legs** long and strongly-boned. **Feet** cat-feet. **Tail** docked. **Coat** wire-haired, bristly eyebrows and beard.

Character calm, faithful, undaunted defender.

86

Height at withers:
14–20 inches
(35½–51 cm).
Colour: yellow in
several shades, deer-
red, black, brown.
White markings are
usual.

87

Height at withers:
about 18 inches
(45 cm).
Colour: black,
chestnut, black
markings, dark brown,
grey with red or tan
markings, pepper and
salt.

88

Height at withers:
28 inches (71 cm).
Colour: black, pepper
and salt.

89 Rottweiler

Origin the name comes from Rottweil in Germany, a Roman settlement which became a free town in the thirteenth century and has always been a meeting-place for cattle dealers. This breed of cattle drovers, originally created for boat hunting, is supposed to carry the blood of Roman cattle dogs, Molossian Hounds, fighting dogs, Brabanter Bullenbeiszer and indigenous sheep-herding dogs. The Rottweiler was used not only to drive and protect the herds but was often the guardian of his masters purse which he wore upon his collar. Later the breed was used as a draught dog and for police work.

Appearance Head wide skull of medium length, broad muzzle as long as the skull, marked stop. Eyes dark with a good-natured, self-confident expression. Ears small, triangular drop ears. Neck strong, round and broad, without throatiness. Body rather short with broad, deep chest and well-sprung ribs. Legs moderately long, strongly-boned. Feet round, hindfeet somewhat longer than the forefeet. Tail docked. Coat coarse and short.

Character affectionate, intelligent, obedient, willing work dog, excellent defender.

90 Saint Bernard (Bernhardiner)

Origin old Swiss watch-dogs, descended from the Roman Molossus, came to the Monastery of Saint Bernard in the Alps and proved to be excellently fitted to tracking lost or hurt travellers. Originally short-haired, those dogs were crossed for purposes of blood-renewal with the long-haired Newfoundland; the result was the long-haired Saint Bernard.

Appearance Head broad skull with distinct stop, short muzzle which should be deeper than it is long. Eyes moderately large, brown or hazel. the lower eyelid has a light haw; the expression is intelligent and friendly. Ears drop ears, triangular and moderately large. Neck strong and slightly-arched with well-developed dewlaps. Body well-sprung ribs and a broad, straight back. Legs straight, strongly-boned and muscled. Feet broad with well-arched toes. Tail long and, in the long-coated variety, well-feathered. Coat very close, short and hard, and in the long-haired variety, moderately long.

Character quiet, friendly, reliable.

91 Samojedskaja (Samoyed)

Origin the nomadic tribes of the Samoyed in the Russian Tundra regions possessed large herds of reindeer which were guarded by dogs now called Samoyed; these dogs also had to draw sleighs, bear burdens and assist the hunters. Originally their lives were closely linked with those of their owners and they slept in their huts. This is a Russian breed, but the FCI recognized the standards set up in England.

Appearance Head wedge-shaped, with wide skull, medium sized muzzle, slight stop. Eyes deep set, dark, with a lively, intelligent expression. Ears not too long prick ears with rounded tips. Neck moderately long and strong. Body of medium length with broad, deep chest and well-sprung ribs. Legs moderately long with good bones. Feet long and somewhat flat. Tail long and carried curled over the back. Coat hard, long and straight, and stands out well from the body through a dense, short undercoat.

Character lively, trustworthy, intelligent.

89

Height at withers:
dog: 24–27 inches
(61–68½ cm), bitch:
22–26 inches
(56–66 cm).
Colour: black with
mahogany to light
brown markings.

90

Height at withers:
dog: at least 28 inches
(71 cm), bitch: at least
26 inches (66 cm).
The taller the better.
Colour: white and red;
red and white,
brindle patches with
white markings. The
breast, the feet, the
blaze, the tip of the tail
and the collar should
be white.

91

Height at withers:
dog: from 21 inches
(53½ cm), bitch: from
18 inches (45½ cm).
Colour: white, cream,
biscuit; self-coloured
or multi-coloured, the
white as well as the
colour and the patches
should be pure.

92 Sanshu

Origin bred in the Aichi region from the Chow Chow and the indigenous dogs early this century, this breed has now spread all over Japan.
Appearance Head fairly wide skull, strong, short muzzle, little stop. Eyes almond-shaped, dark. Ears small, triangular prick ears. Neck rather short. Body not too short, with deep chest and well-sprung ribs. Legs of moderate length and strongly-boned. Feet oval. Tail curled. Coat moderately long, hard and coarse, with dense undercoat.
Character intelligent, lively, good watch-dog.

93 Schnauzer

Origin the present Schnauzer developed in Würtemberg, Germany, and is supposed to originate from the medieval Biberhund and two old and wide-spread indigenous types of dogs—the rough-haired companions of the waggoners, and the ratters which were very much appreciated in the house and the farmyard.
Appearance Head rather long, not too wide skull, long, strong muzzle, marked stop. Eyes oval and dark. Ears cropped. Neck fairly long, without throatiness. Body short with moderately broad, deep chest and flat ribs. Legs moderately long with strong bones. Feet short and round. Tail docked to three joints. Coat wire-haired; beard and bristly eyebrows are particular characteristics.
Character lively, affectionate, intelligent, tireless, distrustful of strangers, good with children, responsive to training.

94 Sennenhund, Appenzeller (Appenzell Mountain Dog)

Origin developed in other parts of Switzerland, the Toggenburg valleys and around St Gall, as well as in Appenzell, this variety of Sennenhund has been well preserved, although it was first described as late as 1898. It is valued by the peasants for all kinds of farmwork and as a watch-dog for house and yard.
Appearance Head rather broad skull, not too long wedge-shaped muzzle, with marked stop. Eyes rather small and brown, with an intelligent expression. Ears small, triangular drop ears. Neck short and thick. Body broad, deep chest with well-sprung ribs. Legs not too long with strong bones. Feet short and round. Tail of medium length and carried curled. Coat short, hard, dense and glossy.
Character lively, faithful, diligent, good watch-dog, responsive to training.

92

Height at withers:
Large type: dog: 20–22 inches (51–56 cm), bitch: 18–20 inches (45½–51 cm); small type: dog: 16–18 inches (40½–45½ cm), bitch: 15–17 inches (38–43 cm).
Colour: rust-red, black and tan, red, black, light brown, pepper and salt, white with patches.

93

Height at withers: dog: about 20 inches (51 cm), bitch: about 18 inches (45½ cm).
Colour: black, pepper and salt.

94

Height at withers: dog: about 22 inches (56 cm), bitch: about 20 inches (51 cm).
Colour: black with red markings on the cheeks, above the eyes and on the four legs. White blaze, feet and tip of tail and white cross on the breasts.

95 Sennenhund, Berner (Bernese Mountain Dog)

Origin once the most popular dog in central Switzerland, for a time it was superseded by imported breeds, especially the German Shepherd Dog, but made a come-back after 1900. The breed now enjoys great popularity in Switzerland and elsewhere.

Appearance Head broad skull, strong, medium-sized muzzle, slight stop. **Eyes** dark brown with a kind expression. **Ears** short, triangular drop ears. **Neck** rather short. **Body** short rather than long, with deep, broad chest and well-sprung ribs. **Legs** of medium length and strongly-boned. **Feet** round. **Tail** long. **Coat** long, soft and straight or slightly wavy.

Character dignified, affectionate, good watch-dog, responsive to training.

96 Sennenhund, Entlebucher (Entlebuch Mountain Dog)

Origin the last of the four Swiss mountain dogs to recover popularity was the Entlebucher from the valleys of the Emme and the Entle in the Cantons of Lucerne and Berne.

Appearance Head rather broad skull, moderately long, strong muzzle, slight stop. **Eyes** fairly small, brown, with a lively and kind expression. **Ears** drop ears. **Neck** short and thick. **Body** rather long with deep, broad chest. **Legs** rather short and strong. **Feet** round. **Tail** congenitally short, long or medium, both the latter are docked. **Coat** short, hard and glossy.

Character calm, intelligent, kind, trustworthy, good watch-dog, responsive to training.

97 Sennenhund, Grosser Schweizer (Great Swiss Mountain Dog)

Origin once popular in the whole of Switzerland, where it was often used to haul light carts, this breed was threatened with extinction from which it was saved at the start of the twentieth century.

Appearance Head broad skull with a muzzle of equal length, slight stop. **Eyes** of medium size, from hazel to chestnut brown, with a lively and intelligent expression. **Ears** medium-sized, triangular, drop ears. **Neck** moderately long, with broad, deep chest and well-sprung ribs. **Legs** rather long, strongly-boned. **Feet** round and short; the dew claw should be removed. **Tail** long. **Coat** 1–2 inches (2½–5 cm) long, hard, with undercoat.

Character faithful, good with children, good watch-dog, responsive to training as a rescue dog.

95
Height at withers:
dog: 26 inches
(66 cm), bitch: about
24 inches (61 cm).
Colour: similar to that
of the Appenzeller
Sennenhund.

96
Height at withers:
dog: up to 22 inches
(56 cm), bitch:
18½–20 inches
(46½–51 cm).
Colour: similar to that
of the Appenzeller
Sennenhund.

97
Height at withers:
dog: 26–28 inches
(66–71 cm), bitch:
24–26 inches
(61–66 cm).
Colour: similar to that
of the Appenzeller
Sennenhund.

98 Siberian Husky

Origin originally the dogs which we call Huskies were used by the Chukchi, a nomadic Arctic people who live in the basin of the Kolyma river and at the foot of the Cherski Mountains. It is a very ancient breed, which is becoming more and more popular outside its native country.

Appearance Head rather narrow between the ears and the moderately long muzzle equals the length of the skull; slight stop. Eyes brown or blue, one brown and one blue eye are permissible but not desirable. Ears medium sized prick ears. Neck rather short. Body of moderate length and not compact. Legs medium sized with strong bones. Feet oval. Tail long and carried over the back. Coat of medium length, soft and very thick, with a dense soft, fluffy undercoat which should not be too short.

Character docile, affectionate, kind.

99 Tibetan Mastiff

Origin in the steppes of central Asia and the foothills of the Himalayas this centuries-old breed is used for herding yaks and guarding houses and tents.

Appearance Head large, with a wide skull, short, broad muzzle, marked stop. Eyes brown and deep set. Ears small, heart-shaped drop ears. Neck compact, with throatiness. Body short, with a rather deep, broad chest. Legs rather long, strongly-boned. Feet large and short. Tail long and curled sideways. Coat long and straight, with dense, thick undercoat.

Character calm, docile, attached to its owner, not friendly towards everybody, good watch-dog.

100 Tosa (Japanese Fighting Dog)

Origin specially bred during the Meiji period (1868–1912) for dog-fights which were then very popular. The original fighting dogs, bred in the Kochi district, were crossed with the Mastiff, the Bulldog, the Bull Terrier, the Great Dane and the Saint Bernard.

Appearance Head broad skull, moderately long and broad muzzle, marked stop. Eyes rather small, with a vicious expression, red-brown. Ears small drop ears. Neck rather long and strong, with much throatiness. Body deep, broad chest with well-sprung ribs. Legs rather long. Coat short, hard, coarse and dense.

Character courageous, patient, gentle, good watch-dog.

98

Height at withers:
dog: 21–23½ inches
(53½–59 cm), bitch:
20–22 inches
(51–56 cm).
Colour: all colours and
white and all markings
allowed. Different
shades of grey, tan and
black with white
markings are most
usual. The cap-like
mask and spectacles
are typical.

99

Height at withers:
dog: 25–27 inches
(63½–68½ cm), bitch:
22–24 inches
(56–61 cm).
Colour: black, black
with tan markings,
golden.

100

Height at withers:
dog: above 24 inches
(61 cm), bitch: above
22 inches (56 cm).
Colour: all tan, tan
markings on white or
on a base of a different
colour.

101 Grönlandshund

Origin akin to the Eskimo Dog, the Alaskan Malamute, the Husky and the Samoyed. These sleigh-dogs, probably originated in east Siberia, occur in Greenland, Labrador, Alaska and northern Canada and the different types were recognized as separate breeds not long ago. The Greenland Dog is the most pure.
Appearance similar to that of the Eskimo Dog. **Height at withers** a little less than the Eskimo Dog. **Colour** never solid white.

102 Perro de Presa Mallorquin (Majorcan Bulldog)

Origin Majorca.
Appearance **Head** large, skull broad and square, the muzzle short and broad, marked stop. **Neck** long and heavy. **Body** of medium length with a deep, round chest. **Legs** moderately long and strongly-boned. **Feet** round with dew claws. **Tail** long. **Coat** short and soft. **Height at withers** 23 inches (58½ cm). **Colour** brindle, preferably with little white.
Character intrepid.

103 Shika Inu

Origin in former times used in the mountainous regions of Japan for deer hunting, it has now become a house- and watch-dog.
Appearance resembles the Akita Inu but is smaller. **Height at withers** 18–22 inches (45–55 cm). **Colour** pepper and salt, red-grey, black-grey, black, white.
Character affectionate, lively, intelligent.

Terriers

The name terrier comes from *terra*, the Latin word for earth, and these dogs were originally used to hunt badgers and foxes, driving or digging them out of the holes in which they had gone to earth. When the terriers could not succeed in this, they would indicate the whereabouts of the animal, making it easier for the hunter to dig it out. This work demanded sturdy, courageous dogs of small to medium size. The name terrier came to be applied to all dogs used to destroy harmful rodents and most terriers are still excellent catchers of rats and mice. It is generally thought that the Old English Rough-haired Black and Tan Terrier was the ancestor of all the terrier breeds. These dogs were used more than two hundred years ago to hunt foxes and otters.

The different kinds of soil, landscapes and game on which the dogs were used varied the requirements which they had to meet. In order to obtain the special hunting qualities desired, hound breeds were used for crossing, whereas for an altogether different kind of work, such as bull-baiting and fighting, terriers were crossed with mastiffs. The name of the locality or county where the breed originated can be identified from many of the breed names.

Terriers came into fashion in the second half of the nineteenth century, when dog shows were started, as a result of which standards were set. At first, working qualities only were aimed at, but nowadays full attention is also given to the outward appearance. The popularity of terriers has been growing ever since their first appearance at shows, and since the First World War it has become much more widespread. They are now to be found all over the world. Terriers are temperamental and lively dogs who are in their element with young people and in a noisy family. They are strong and playful, so that they are excellent companions for older children, with whom they find the opportunity to expand their great energy. It is a mistake to believe that the smaller representatives of this group should be lap dogs.

Twenty-two of the thirty acknowledged terrier breeds originated in England; six breeds were developed from English breeds; one in Germany, one in Czechoslovakia, two in Australia, one in Japan and one in the United States. One of the Australian, as well as the English toy terrier breeds, belongs to the group of small companion dogs, whereas the Boston Terrier and the Japanese Terrier belong to the group of large companion dogs.

The Tibetan Terrier is not a terrier at all and is probably related to the sheep-herding dogs.

Terrier breeds may be short- or long-legged, the former almost never being short-haired. Tails are usually docked and ears are never cropped. The wire-haired breeds require much more attention than the short-haired ones. Whereas a daily brush-up and a professional trim twice a year are sufficient for a house-pet, it is quite another matter for a show dog. Nowadays, a badly prepared dog does not have a chance at a show, whatever his qualities may be. Long before the show and until the very moment he enters the ring, full attention is given to his grooming, and it goes without saying that much professional skill and a full knowledge of the breed are needed to make a wire-haired dog ready for show. On the other hand, the wire-haired breeds have an advantage over the short-haired: skilful dressing makes it possible to camouflage shortcomings and to accentuate the good points of the dog. In any case, the looks of a terrier after trimming are quite different from those of a dog in full coat; a careful grooming gives him a strong-lined and striking appearance.

Scale of Terrier illustrations 1 :10

104 Airedale Terrier

Origin the valley of the River Aire in Yorkshire. It was bred for the hunting of otters by crossing the Old English Terrier with the Otterhound and the Welsh Harrier.

Appearance Head long, not too broad, with flat cheeks and little stop. **Eyes** dark, lively and intelligent expression. **Ears** small and V-shaped drop ears, placed high at the sides of the head. **Neck** clean, of moderate length and thickness with no excessive loose skin. **Body** short, muscular and strong with the chest deep but not broad. **Legs** long and well-boned. **Feet** small and round. **Tail** should not be docked too short. **Coat** harsh and wiry with a shorter and smooth undercoat; needs regular trimming.

Character active, affectionate, amenable to training.

105 Australian Terrier

Origin bred from several English terriers, including the Yorkshire, Cairn and Dandie Dinmont, which were repeatedly crossed with the Australian Silky Terrier.

Appearance Head long with flat, moderately wide skull and slight stop. **Eyes** dark, small and keen. **Ears** pricked, small and short-haired. **Neck** moderately long. **Body** rather long in proportion to the height. **Legs:** rather short. **Feet** small with black or very dark nails. **Tail** docked. **Coat** hard and straight, about 2 inches (5 cm) long; the topknot is soft.

Character clever, affectionate, willing to please.

106 Bedlington Terrier

Origin Rothbury Forest in Northumberland in England. It is named after the village of Bedlington. The Bedlington and the Dandie Dinmont Terriers are believed to have a linked ancestry. They carry hound blood, perhaps from the Otterhound, or more likely from the Greyhound or Whippet.

Appearance Head pear shaped with narrow, rounded skull and without stop, forming a straight line from the occiput to the end of the nose. **Eyes** small, deep set and seem triangular. **Ears** low set, medium large and shaped like a hazelnut. **Neck** long, tapering and deep at the base, with no excessive loose skin. **Body** muscular with flat ribs, deep chest and roached back, the loins markedly arched. **Legs** moderately long. **Feet** long and shaped like a hare's. **Tail** moderate length, thick, low set and tapering to a point. **Coat** thick and linty, with a tendency to twist. On the skull and tips of the ears it is profuse, silky and nearly white.

Character very brave, good fighter, obedient.

104
Height at withers:
dog: about 23–24
inches (58½–61 cm),
bitch: about 22–23
inches (56–58 cm).
Colour: head, legs up
to thighs and elbows:
tan. Body: black or
dark grizzle.

105
Height at withers:
about 10 inches
(25½ cm).
Colour: the body blue,
steel blue or dark
grey-blue with tan on
legs and face; the
topknot blue or silver,
sandy or red allowed.

106
Height at withers:
dog: about 16 inches
(40½ cm), bitches may
be somewhat smaller.
Colour: blue, blue and
tan, liver or sandy.

107 Border Terrier

Origin and use the border country between England and Scotland, where the Bedlington and the Dandie Dinmont come from. Some people think it is the ancestor of these breeds. It has always been and still is a true working dog, which is unrivalled in its ability to drive the fox out of its lair.

Appearance Head should look like that of an otter; it is moderately broad in the skull with short, strong muzzle. **Eyes** dark with a keen expression. **Ears** small, V-shaped drop-ears. **Neck** strong and moderately long. **Body** should be deep, narrow and fairly long. **Legs** moderately long and not heavily boned. **Feet** small. **Tail** moderately short. **Coat** harsh, dense and it has a close undercoat.

Character brave, adaptable, good with children.

108 Bull Terrier

Origin Birmingham, England, where it was produced by crossing old fighting dogs, who carried Bulldog and terrier blood with the Old White English Terrier and the Dalmatian. Later, still more breeds were bred in:

Appearance Head should be long, strong, deep, without hollows and down-faced. **Eyes** dark, narrow, triangular, deep set and slanting with a keen expression. **Ears** pricked, small and thin. **Neck** long, very muscular and without excess skin. **Body** very deep with barrel ribs, wide chest and a short, strong back. **Legs** moderately long with strong round bones. **Feet** round. **Coat** short, harsh and it has a fine gloss.

Character pugnacious, intelligent, lively, well-balanced, obedient.

109 Miniature Bull Terrier

Identical to the Bull Terrier except for size. **Height at withers** not more than 14 inches (35½ cm).

110 Cairn Terrier

Origin and use Highlands of Scotland. Bred for the hunting of otter, fox and badger. 'Cairns' are heaps of boulders in the areas where the terriers were bred to pursue game. This special work called for small fierce dogs who knew how to use their strong teeth.

Appearance Head broad in proportion to its size with a distinct stop and strong, moderately long muzzle. **Eyes** wide-set, sunken, of medium size and dark hazel coloured with shaggy brows. **Ears** prick ears. **Neck** should not be short. **Body** compact with strong, medium long back and deep chest. **Legs** rather short with strong bones. **Forefeet** larger than the hind-feet; they may be slightly turned out. **Tail** short, well furnished and carried gaily. **Coat** profuse, hard upper hair with a short thick, soft undercoat.

Character active, courageous, good-natured.

107
Weight: dog:
13–15½ lb (6–7 kg),
bitch: 11½–14 lb
(5–6 kg).
Colour: red, wheaten,
grizzle and tan or
blue and tan.

108
Height at withers:
there are no limits
either for size or
weight.
Colour: pure white,
head markings
permissible; or
predominately
coloured.

110
Height at withers:
9½–10 inches
(24–25½ cm) or a
little more.
Colour: red, sandy,
grey, brindle; dark ears
and muzzle are typical.

111 Čzesky Terrier (Bohemian Terrier)

Origin and use bred in Bohemia especially for work underground by crossing Scottish and Sealyham Terriers.

Appearance Head moderately broad and rather long. **Eyes** dark. **Ears** moderately large drop ears. **Neck** long. **Body** not too long with well-sprung ribs. **Legs** short. **Feet** round. **Tail** 7–8 inches (18–20½ cm) long. **Coat** wavy with a silky sheen.

Character not aggressive without reason, considerable initiative, good companion in the house and with children.

112 Dandie Dinmont Terrier

Origin and use working dogs from the border country between England and Scotland, akin to the Border and Bedlington Terriers, and, like them, carries hound blood. The name comes from a character in a novel by Sir Walter Scott who kept a pack of these dogs.

Appearance Head large, the skull almost square and the muzzle deep and about 3 inches (7½ cm) long. **Eyes** large, round, dark brown; they have a lively expression. **Ears** pendulous, set low and well back. **Neck** very muscular and strong. **Body** long and deep with well-sprung ribs. The back, low at the shoulders, has a pronounced arch over the loins. **Legs** short and heavily-boned, the hindlegs a little longer than the forelegs. **Feet** hindfeet should be much smaller than front. **Tail** rather short and covered on the upper side with wiry hair of a darker colour than that of the body and light and not so wiry on the underside, the hair getting shorter as it nears the tip. **Coat** 2 inches (5 cm) long, a mixture of hardish and soft hair, lighter in colour and softer on the underpart of the body. The whole is covered with light, soft, silky hair forming a large tuft.

Character quiet, brave, affectionate, good house dog.

113 Deutscher Jagdterrier (German Hunting Terrier)

Origin and use bred by sportsmen in Bavaria by crossing Smooth and Wire Fox Terriers, a Welsh Terrier bitch and a sire who was a direct descendant of the Old English Broken-haired Terrier. A very tough and fierce hunting dog.

Appearance Head a flat skull, wide between the ears with a slight stop and a long, strong muzzle. **Eyes** dark, small and deep set with a resolute expression. **Ears** medium size, V-shaped drop ears and set high. **Neck** rather long. **Body** of moderate length with a straight back and well-sprung ribs. **Legs** moderately long and strongly-boned. **Feet** not too round, with the forefeet broader than the hindfeet. **Tail** docked. **Coat** should lie close to the body; it is dense and smooth.

Character fierce, attentive, distrustful of strangers.

111

Height at withers: 11–14 inches (28–35½ cm).
Colour: the basic colour is grey-blue or light coffee-brown; yellow, grey or white markings allowed on cheeks, underside of the muzzle, neck, breast and belly and in addition on lower parts of legs and under the tail. White collar and tail tip are also permissible, but the basic colour must be prominent.

112

Height at withers: 8–11 inches (20–28 cm).
Colour: pepper (ranging from a dark bluish black to a light silvery-grey) or mustard (reddish brown to pale fawn).

113

Height at withers: not above 16 inches (40½ cm).
Colour: black, black-grey or dark brown; tan markings above eyes, on the muzzle, chest, legs and under the tail.

114 Fox Terrier, Smooth

Origin and use old breed, of which the origin is not clear, used with foxhound packs to drive the fox out of its lair or undergrowth where it cannot be reached by the larger hounds.

Appearance Head a flat, rather narrow skull, very slight stop and long, strong muzzle. **Eyes** dark, small, deep set and round, with a mischievous expression. **Ears** drop ears, small and moderately thick. **Neck** long, well-curved and free from surplus skin. **Body** a deep, but not too broad, chest and very short back. **Legs** strong and not too long. **Feet** small and round. **Tail** should be upright and set on rather high. **Coat** smooth, short, harsh and dense.

Character happy, lively, affectionate, faithful, intelligent.

115 Fox Terrier, Wire

Identical to the Smooth Fox Terrier, but has a very different silhouette because of the longer and harsher coat, especially on the legs and muzzle.

116 Glen of Imaal Terrier

Origin and use an Irish breed originated in County Wicklow in the glen from which it takes its name. A breed of hard workers, not show-dogs, developed to hunt the fox and badger and to fight other dogs.

Appearance Head long and rather broad, with a strong muzzle and pronounced stop. **Eyes** brown with an intelligent expression. **Ears** thin drop ears. **Neck** moderately long. **Body** long with a broad chest and well-sprung ribs. **Legs** short and strongly-boned; the front legs may be slightly bowed. **Feet** almost round and turned slightly outwards. **Tail** docked and carried high. **Coat** harsh but soft rather than wiry and moderately long.

Character very courageous, daredevil, obedient and very attached to his owner.

114
Weight: 16–18 lb
(7–8 kg).
Colour: black and
white, tan and white,
with the white
predominating, or all
white; brindle, red or
liver are objectionable.

115
Height at withers:
dog: should not
exceed 15½ inches
(39 cm), bitch:
proportionately
smaller.
Colour: white should
be predominate; brindle red, liver or
slaty blue markings are
objectionable.

116
Height at withers:
should not exceed
14 inches (35½ cm).
Colour: blue, blue and
tan or wheaten.

117 Irish Terrier

Origin ancestry includes the Old Wire-haired Black and Tan Terrier and a stock of large wheaten terriers from the area around Cork and Ballymena in Ireland.

Appearance Head long with a flat, rather narrow skull, the stop hardly visible, and a long strong muzzle. **Eyes** small, dark hazel and full of life and intelligence. **Ears** small, Vishaped, drop ears. **Neck** should be of fair length and have no surplus skin. **Body** moderately long, and deep with fair spring of ribs. **Legs** moderately long with strong round bones. **Feet** are tolerably round and moderately small. **Tail** generally docked to about three-quarter length. **Coat** hard and wiry and not so long that it obscures the silhouette, with an undercoat of finer, softer hair.

Character good tempered, active, daredevil, affectionate, excellent guard dog.

118 Kerry Blue Terrier

Origin and use south and west Ireland. Used for hunting otter, fox and badger.

Appearance Head strong with a rather long muzzle and slight stop. **Eyes** dark or hazel and small. **Ears** small, thin drop ears. **Neck** moderately long. **Body** short with deep chest and well-sprung ribs. **Legs** moderately long with powerful bones. **Feet** small and round with black nails. **Coat** soft and silky, profuse and wavy and it does not shed. Therefore it requires regular trimming.

Character pugnacious, affectionate, responsive to training.

119 Lakeland Terrier

Origin and use the Lake District of England. Bred for hunting fox and rodents on foot with the pack.

Appearance Head a flat skull and a broad, moderately long muzzle. **Eyes** dark or hazel. **Ears** moderately small, V-shaped, drop ears. **Neck** long. **Body** a reasonably narrow chest and moderately short back. **Legs** rather long. **Feet** small and round. **Tail** moderately long. **Coat** dense and harsh with a good undercoat.

Character brave, friendly, excellent guard dog.

117

Height at withers:
approximately 18
inches (45½ cm).
Colour: bright red, red
wheaten or yellow
red, always
whole-coloured.

118

Height at withers:
dog: 18–19 inches
(45½–48½ cm), bitch:
slightly less.
Colour: any shade of
blue.

119

Height at withers:
should not exceed
14½ inches (37 cm).
Colour: black and tan,
blue and tan, red,
wheaten, red greyish,
liver, blue or black.

119

120 Manchester Terrier (formerly Black and Tan Terrier)

Origin and use probably the result of crossing the Old English Broken-haired Black and Tan Terrier, and the extinct White English Terrier which, except for colour, it greatly resembles. About 1870 the breed was used at rat catching contests at which there was heavy betting.

Appearance Head long and wedge-shaped with a flat skull. **Eyes** dark, small and oval with a mischievous expression. **Ears** small, V-shaped drop ears. **Neck** long. **Body** short with a narrow, deep chest and well-sprung ribs. **Legs** moderately long. **Feet** small, midway between hare-feet and cat-feet. **Tail** short, fairly thick, tapering and carried level with the back. **Coat** dense, short and very glossy.

Character lively, sometimes stubborn, a fierce rodent catcher, friendly.

121 Norfolk Terrier

Origin as that of the Norwich Terrier. In 1964 the English Kennel Club decided to consider the Norwich Terrier with drop ears as a separate breed, which was named the Norfolk Terrier.

Appearance identical to that of the Norwich Terrier except for the drop ears.

Character as that of the Norwich Terrier.

122 Norwich Terrier

Origin bred at Norwich by crossing small red terriers from East Anglia with other terrier breeds.

Appearance Head a broad, slightly rounded skull with a good stop and a strong and 'foxy' muzzle. **Eyes** dark, keen and full of expression. **Ears** prick ears. **Neck** short and strong. **Body** short and compact with well-sprung ribs. **Legs** short and strong. **Feet** round. **Tail** medium docked. **Coat** lies close to the body and is hard and wiry; on the head it is short and smooth but forms a full neck ruff.

Character indefatigable, energetic, happy.

(In the United States the breed includes the drop eared variety now known in England as the Norfolk Terrier.)

120

Height at withers:
dog: 16 inches
(40½ cm) desirable,
bitch: 15 inches
(38 cm).
Colour: black with tan
markings exactly
placed. There must be
a black mark above the
feet and pencilling on
the toes.

121

Height at withers:
10 inches (25½ cm).
Colour: red, black
and tan or grizzle.

122

Height at withers:
10 inches (25 cm).
Colour: red, black
and tan or grizzle.

123 Scottish Terrier

Origin and use the north of Scotland in the Aberdeen district where it was used to destroy foxes and rodents.

Appearance Head long with a flat skull and slight stop. **Eyes** dark and almond shaped. **Ears** pointed, prick ears. **Neck** moderately long. **Body** a deep chest, well-sprung ribs and a proportionately short back. **Legs** short and strongly-boned. **Feet** of good size. **Tail** of moderate length, thick at the root and tapering to the tip. **Coat** harsh, dense and wiry with a short, dense and soft undercoat.

Character independent, vigilant, intelligent.

124 Sealyham Terrier

Origin and use Sealyham House near Haverfordwest in Pembrokeshire, Wales, where, in order to obtain a small dog which could successfully hunt otter, fox and badger, Captain Edwards crossed short-legged white terriers, of a strain that possibly came from Flanders, with other breeds, probably the Dandie Dinmont and the Bull Terrier.

Appearance Head a broad, slightly arched skull with a long square muzzle. **Eyes** dark, moderately large and round. In America, Australia and some continental countries, dark eye rims are preferred. **Ears** moderately large drop ears, slightly rounded at the tip. **Neck** rather long and thick. **Body** moderately long with well-sprung ribs and a deep, broad chest. **Legs** short and strong. **Feet** cat-like. **Tail** short and carried erect. **Coat** long, hard and wiry.

Character faithful, intelligent, happy. Despite their natural obstinacy they can be trained to become obedient.

125 Skye Terrier

Origin and use the Isle of Skye and the north-west of Scotland. The origin of this very old breed is obscure but it was bred to hunt foxes, polecats, martens, otters and badgers.

Appearance Head long and not too broad with a strong muzzle and slight stop. **Eyes** dark brown or hazel and moderately large. **Ears** can be prick or drop ears. The former should be erect and fairly small, the latter larger and lying close to the head. **Neck** long. **Body** long and low with well-sprung ribs and a deep chest. **Legs** short and muscular. **Feet** long and pointed. **Tail** long and feathered. **Coat** long, hard and straight with a short, close undercoat that is soft and woolly.

Character one-man dog, distrustful of strangers, faithful and intelligent.

123

Height at withers:
10–11 inches
(25½–28 cm).
Colour: black,
wheaten or brindle.

124

Height at withers:
should not exceed 12
inches (30½ cm).
Colour: mostly all
white, or with lemon,
brown or badger pied
markings on head
and ears.

125

Height at withers:
10 inches (25½ cm).
Colour: blue-grey is
most normal but all
colours are permitted;
the nose must be
black.

126 Soft-coated Wheaten Terrier

Origin the southern counties of Munster from which this oldest of the Irish terrier breeds spread all over Ireland to become the ancestor of several of the better known terriers.

Appearance Head moderately long with a flat-topped skull, pronounced stop and a strong muzzle which should be of the same length as the skull. **Eyes** dark hazel and of medium size. **Ears** small, drop ears. **Neck** moderately long and without loose skin. **Body** short with a deep chest and well-sprung ribs. **Legs** of moderate length with strong bones. **Feet** small. **Tail** docked short. **Coat** abundant and soft, with waves or curls.

Character energetic, companionable, good cattle dog and watch dog.

127 Staffordshire Bull Terrier

Origin and use result of crossing the Bulldog and terrier and the ancestor of the white and coloured Bull Terrier. A fighting dog, originally used for baiting bulls and bears; when this was prohibited the dogs were secretly used to fight one another.

Appearance Head short and deep with a broad skull, very pronounced cheek muscles, a distinct stop and a short muzzle. **Eyes** preferably dark, round and moderately large. **Ears** rose (small, thin and folded inwards at the back) or half-pricked and not too large. **Neck** rather short. **Body** short with a deep, broad chest and well-sprung ribs. **Legs** not too long and set wide apart. **Feet** medium sized. **Tail** of medium length. **Coat** smooth, short and dense.

Character courageous, intelligent, tenacious, affectionate, calm, good with children.

128 Welsh Terrier

Origin old breed originally used to hunt mountain foxes and to run with the Otterhound pack in Wales.

Appearance Head a flat, moderately narrow skull with a slight stop and rather long muzzle. **Eyes** small, dark hazel and have a courageous expression. **Ears** small drop ears, carried forward and close to the cheek. **Neck** long and slightly arched. **Body** short; moderately broad chest. **Legs** of moderate length with strong bones. **Feet** small and cat-like. **Tail** docked, not too short. **Coat** profuse, dense, hard and wiry.

Character quiet, happy, clever.

126
Height at withers:
up to 18 inches
(45½ cm).
Colour: clear wheaten.

127
Height at withers:
14–16 inches
(35½–40½ cm).
Colour: red, fawn,
white, black, blue or
brindle, or one of
these colours with
white.

128
Height at withers:
should not exceed
15½ inches (39½ cm).
Colour: black and tan
or black-grizzle and
tan.

129 West Highland Terrier

Origin unwanted white puppies in litters of the Cairn Terrier out of which this dog was bred.

Appearance Head a slightly arched skull, a distinct stop and a slightly tapering muzzle with a large black nose. **Eyes** wide set, dark, medium size, keen and intelligent. **Ears** small, pointed prick ears. **Neck** rather long. **Body** compact with a deep chest and well-sprung ribs. **Legs** short and strong. **Feet** round with the forefeet larger than the hindfeet. **Tail** 5–6 inches (13–15 cm) long. **Coat** long, hard and straight with a short, soft, dense undercoat.

Character happy, eager to learn, affectionate, tolerant.

130 Amertoy Terrier

Origin smooth-haired terriers were crossed in the United States with the dwarf Black and Tan Terrier and the Chihuahua. The resulting breed has not yet been recognized by the American Kennel Club.

Appearance resembling a small Smooth-haired Fox Terrier, but with more arched skull and prick ears. The chest is broader and rounder. **Weight** 4½–8 lb (2–3½ kg). **Colour** all colours allowed, except all white or all black. Generally white with black and orange.

131 Jack Russell Terrier

Origin Great Britain. The Reverend John (Jack) Russell from Devonshire bred a stock of hunt terriers by crossing low white terriers with Old Jack, the ancestor of the Fox Terrier. Recognition was never asked for this breed.

Appearance resembling a coarse Fox Terrier with shorter legs (smooth varieties are also common).

Height at withers: about 14 inches (35½ cm).

132 Japanese Terrier

Origin Kobe and Yokohama. Bred from indigenous dogs crossed with short-haired terriers.

Appearance square and short haired, tip ears and docked tail.

Height at withers: 12–15 inches (30½–38 cm). **Colour** white with black and brown markings.

133 Staffordshire Terrier (Yankee Terrier, Pit Dog Bull Terrier, American Bull Terrier)

Origin the United States, where the breed was recognized by the American Kennel Club in 1936 and finally called Staffordshire Terrier, although cross-breeding with the Staffordshire Bull Terrier was accepted.

Appearance larger and heavier than the Staffordshire Bull Terrier. Cropped as well as uncropped ears allowed. **Height at withers** 18–19 inches (45½–48 cm). **Colour** any colour allowed but all white, more than eighty per cent white, black and tan and liver not encouraged.

Character exceedingly courageous.

129

Height at withers:
about 11 inches
(28 cm).
Colour: pure white

Hounds and greyhounds

The characteristic common to all the breeds included in this group is that they pursué game and, if necessary, prevent its escape, giving the sportsman the opportunity to kill it. Nevertheless, the dogs set to work in differing ways according to their type. The majority of the breeds mentioned in this group are included in the category of hounds. They hunt with their nose to the ground in order to follow the trail, all the while giving tongue until the game is put up and driven before the guns or killed by the pack. The barking of the hounds as soon as they are on the trail is necessary to let the sportsman know their whereabouts and to indicate the spot where he will be able to shoot. Holding the quarry in one place was especially important in earlier times, before guns were known, because the sportsman had to be able to approach the game at close range.

Hunting on horse-back with a pack of hounds for fox, roe buck, deer or wild boar was a very popular pastime with kings and noblemen, first in France and later also in England. The Grands Chiens Courants, kept in large packs on the estates, were bred with the utmost care to obtain the dogs most fit for the terrain and game at hand. As packs of homogeneous outward appearance were wanted, selection also took place for type, colour, size and even sound, because connoisseurs of hounds demanded that the voices of the pack should harmonize. In this way numerous breeds of French hounds were bred which usually had the name of their native locality. Most of these breeds are now extinct, but almost all hounds now in existence carry their blood. The large hounds were used by mounted huntsmen; the smaller types and bassets which were afterwards developed by mutation, were intended for hunting badger, hare and rabbit on foot. The smallest varieties bolt the game out of its lair or hold it at bay.

The famous ancestor of the pack-hounds is the Chien de Saint Hubert, the type with which Saint Hubert hunted in the seventh century. This hound originally occurred in two varieties, the black and tan and the white, called Talbot; the white has been extinct for a long time. The Chien de Saint Hubert was bred for many centuries in the monastery of Andain in the Belgian Ardennes and until 1789 the monks had to yield to the king six hounds every year to be used as trackers. In the nineteenth century, purebred examples of the Chien de Saint Hubert were no longer to be found in either Belgium or France. The breed came to England at the time of the Norman Conquest and the English have kept it pure ever since. After many ups and downs the breed still exists as the Bloodhound, which is meant to suggest 'of pure blood'. Its outward appearance has somewhat altered in the course of time; the original Chien de Saint Hubert was plainer in looks and smaller than the present Bloodhound which has a very long and narrow head with heavily folded skin.

Another category of hounds, the greyhounds, hunt in an altogether different way. They do not use their nose but their eyes and they only take action when they see the game. In some countries, such as Persia and Afghanistan, the sportsman takes the dog with him on his horse and unleashes it when the game is in sight. In the short and swift chase that follows the dog overtakes the quarry and pulls it down. In Russia, the tsars, grand dukes and landed gentry kept many hounds and greyhounds which they used together for hunting wolves. First the hounds tracked down the game and drove it into open country, then light and very swift greyhounds were set loose and had further to pursue the quarry until it lost speed, whereupon Borzois—the 'stranglers'—especially bred sturdier and stronger for this purpose, came in to kill it.

The greyhound breeds with prick ears, all very much akin to each other, are half hounds, half greyhounds. Usually they have a very fine nose, which they use for their work. Their great similarity to the hounds depicted 5,000 years ago on Egyptian monuments suggests that these breeds have been kept very pure through the ages.

Some spitz, pole dogs and two mastiff breeds are included in this group. The first two categories consist of multi-purpose utility dogs and the task of the breeds included in the present group is to assist the sportsman. The Finsk Spets is one of the few, if not the only dog in this category, to be used for hunting feathered game. The dog follows the game until it alights on a branch and then calls the hunter by his barking. The two mastiff breeds have been bred especially for hunting big game.

The breeds discussed above share a gentle and not pugnacious character and all of them are very affectionate towards their own people and aloof with strangers. The two latter qualities are more pronounced in greyhounds than in the other hounds. All hounds are self-willed, which is necessary for dogs who have to do their work very independently, without the assistance or interference of the sportsman. They will seldom, be strictly obedient.

(It should be noted that the expression *Bracke* or *Brak* is used to indicate hounds exclusively in the German and Dutch languages. In all other languages, such as the Franch *Braque* and the Italian *Bracco*, the word means 'gundog', and this often gives rise to misunderstanding.)

Scale of Hound and Greyhound illustrations 1 :15

134 American Foxhound

Origin and use the early ancestors of this breed were taken to Maryland in North America in 1650. Later on they were crossed with dogs imported from England, Ireland and France, in order to obtain the dogs most fitted for American fox-hunting.

Appearance Head long cast with long, moderately broad skull and muzzle, slight stop. **Eyes** brown. **Ears** pendulous and moderately long. **Body** of medium length with a chest more deep than broad and well-sprung ribs. **Legs** long, strongly-boned. **Feet** short. **Tail** long. **Coat** moderately long, dense and hard.

Character not pugnacious, friendly.

135 Ariégeois

Origin and use this breed was originated in the Ariège, in south-west France, by crossing the Briquet with the Grand Gascon-Saintongeois.

Appearance Head dry with long, rather narrow skull with marked occiput, long, rather narrow muzzle, slight stop. **Eyes** dark, without haw, gentle expression. **Ears** thin, not too long, hanging in folds. **Neck** long and light. **Body** moderately long with deep, slightly-arched ribs. **Legs** of medium length, strongly-boned. **Feet** hare-feet. **Tail** long. **Coat** short.

Character gentle, affectionate, strong hunting instinct.

136 Basset Artésien-Normand

Origin and use in 1938 the Société Centrale Canine decided to eliminate the Basset d'Artois and to recognize the Basset Artésien-Normand, which had originated from crossings of the former breed and the already extinct Basset Normand.

Appearance Head lean, long, moderately broad skull; broad, moderately long muzzle, slight stop. **Eyes** large and dark brown with slight haw and a calm, serious expression. **Ears** very long, thin, hanging in folds. **Neck** rather long, little throatiness. **Body** long, moderately deep, broad chest and well-sprung ribs. **Legs** short, crooked, strongly-boned. **Feet** large and short. **Tail** long. **Coat** short and dense.

Character affectionate, faithful, stubborn, happy, strong hunting instinct.

134

Height at withers:
dog: 22–25 inches
(56–63½ cm), bitch:
21–24 inches
(53½–61 cm).
Colour: any hound
colours.

135

Height at withers:
dog: 22–24 inches
(56–61 cm), bitch:
21–23 inches
(53½–58½ cm).
Colour: white and
black, sometimes
mottled. Pale red
markings on cheeks
and above eyes.

136

Height at withers:
10½–14½ inches
(27–37 cm).
Colour: tricolour: red,
especially on the head,
with black, hare or
badger mantle or
specks, and white.
Bicolour: white and
orange.

137 Basset Bleu de Gascogne

Origin and use the name of this breed is misleading because it is not derived from the French district of Gascogny but from the name of one of the breeds from which it originated, the Petit Bleu de Gascogne.

Appearance Head lean, moderately broad, long skull, long and not too narrow muzzle, slight stop. **Eyes** dark brown with a slight haw, loving and somewhat sad expression. **Ears** long, thin, folded and pendulous. **Neck** rather long with slight throatiness. **Body** long, very broad, not too deep in the breast. **Legs** short (the shorter the better) crooked, heavily-boned. **Feet** oval. **Tail** long. **Coat** short and dense.

Character friendly, stubborn, strong hunting instinct.

138 Basset Fauve de Bretagne

Origin and use this breed originated in Brittany, France, and is descended from the Basset Griffon Vendéen.

Appearance Head moderately broad and long skull, moderately long muzzle, slight stop. **Eyes** dark with a lively expression. **Ears** not too long, thin and pendulous. **Neck** rather short. **Body** of moderate length, broad with a fairly deep chest. **Legs** short, heavy, straight or slightly-crooked. **Feet** strong and short. **Tail** long. **Coat** very hard, dense, not too long and almost smooth.

Character lively, enterprising.

139 Basset Griffon Vendéen, Grande Taille

Origin and use bred in the Vendée in south-west France especially for coursing hares. A Briquet is the type of dog usually used for this sport but the landscape of the Vendée is interspersed with hedges and roads which are impassable in winter, so that hunting is not on horseback but on foot. This creates the need for a dog which is less swift than the larger Briquet. **Appearance Head** with not very broad, long cast skull, long muzzle, slight stop. **Eyes** large and dark, with an intelligent expression. **Ears** thin, long and pendulous. **Neck** long and strong without throatiness. **Body** long with a roomy deep chest. **Legs** large and strong. **Tail** long. **Coat** hard, not too long, lies close to the body.

Character self-willed, independent, faithful, one-man dog.

140 Basset Griffon Vendéen, Petite Taille

Origin and use this breed from the Vendée is used by the sportsman on foot for normal basset work, such as trailing and beating game from cover. **Appearance** very similar to that of the Basset Vendéen, Grande Taille, but the **head**, the **ears** and the **body** are comparatively shorter. **Height at withers** 13½–15 inches (34–38 cm).

137

Height at withers:
12–15 inches
(30½–38 cm).
Colour: blue or white
with black spots, with
or without black
mantle; red markings.

138

Height at withers:
13–14½ inches
(33–37 cm).
Colour: golden-
wheaten or fawn with
black point. White spot
on neck or breast
allowed.

139

Height at withers:
15–17 inches
(38–43 cm).
Colour: self-coloured:
fawn with black
points, hare, whitish
grey; bicoloured:
white and black,
white and grey, white
and red; tricoloured:
white, black and red,
white, hare and red,
white, grey and red.

141 Basset Hound

Origin and use the breed was introduced in English dog shows in 1875;
it originated from a cross of the French Basset and the Bloodhound. In later
years, further Bloodhound blood was added and since the Second World
War, Bassets Artésiens-Normands were occasionally used. Only the lighter
types of Basset Hound are fit for work in the pack, the heavier ones are
exclusively show or house dogs.

Appearance Head rather long, with a medium broad skull, not too broad
muzzle, slight stop and loose skin. **Eyes** brown to hazel, the red of the lower
lid shows. **Ears** pendulous, very long, supple, narrow and curl inwards.
Neck rather long with throatiness. **Body** with slightly prominent chestbone,
long, with rather broad, deep chest and well-sprung ribs. **Legs** short,
heavily-boned with the forelegs slightly crooked inwards. **Feet** heavy, forefeet straight or slightly turned outwards. **Tail** long. **Coat** short and smooth.

Character calm, self-willed, affectionate, disobedient.

142 Bayerischer Gebirgsschweisshund
(Bavarian Schweisshund)

Origin and use in Bavaria, at the end of the last century, remnants of
indigenous scent hounds were crossed with Hanoverian scent hounds to
obtain a lighter dog suitable for hunting chamois in the mountains, a task
for which the Hanoverian had proved to be too heavy.

Appearance Head broad skull, not too long, pointed muzzle, slight stop.
Eyes brown, preferably dark. **Ears** slightly more than medium length, heavy
and hanging flat. **Neck** of medium length, without throatiness. **Body** not too
short, with not too broad, deep chest and preferably slightly higher at the
loin than at the withers. **Legs** not too long, strongly-boned. **Feet** oval.
Tail long. **Coat** dense, hard, lying close to the body.

Character lively, intelligent, trustworthy.

143 Beagle

Origin and use old documents prove that Beagles existed in the time of
Henry VIII in England. It is the smallest version of the hunting hound.
A popular house dog in many countries, it is also a very popular hunting dog
in England, the United States and France, where several packs are still kept
for hunting hare on foot.

Appearance Head rather long and medium broad skull, sufficiently long,
broad muzzle with flewed lips and marked stop. **Eyes** brown or hazel, with a
friendly expression. **Ears** thin, fairly long and hanging in a fold. **Neck** of
medium length, with slight throatiness. **Body** short, with deep chest and
well-sprung ribs. **Legs** rather short, strongly-boned. **Feet** round. **Tail** long.
Coat short, dense and coarse. The rough-haired variety has very dense,
wiry hair.

Character friendly, lively, affectionate.

144 Beagle, Pocket

Appearance identical to the Beagle except for the **height at withers** which
is never more than 10 inches (25 cm).

141

Height at withers:
13–15 inches
(33–38 cm).
Colour: generally
black, white and tan or
from very pale to dark
orange and white, but
there is no rigid colour
standard.

142

Height at withers:
dog: should not
exceed 20 inches
(51 cm), bitch: should
not exceed 18 inches
(45½ cm).
Colour: all shades
from red to yellow or
brindle or lightly
speckled.

143

Height at withers:
not below 13 inches
(33 cm), not
exceeding 16 inches
(40½ cm).
Colour: any hound
colour.

145 Berner Laufhund

Origin and use all four Swiss hound breeds, the Bernese, Jura, Lucernese and Swiss, are closely related to the Chien de Saint Hubert and the old French hounds. They are said to have reached Switzerland at the beginning of our era or even earlier. They were saved from extinction in the first half of this century.

Appearance Head long with a rather narrow skull and muzzle, slight stop. **Eyes** should be as dark as possible. **Ears** very long ears hanging in folds. **Neck** rather long, without throatiness. **Body** long, with not too broad, deep chest and slightly-sprung ribs. **Legs** fairly long and well-boned. **Feet** round. **Tail** long. **Coat** dense, moderately short and lying close to the body or wire-haired with a hard, moderately long uppercoat which stands off from the body and a dense, soft, short undercoat.

Character calm, affectionate, gentle.

146 Berner Niederlaufhund

Appearance similar to that of the large size except for the height at withers which is 12–15 inches (30½–38 cm).

147 Billy

Origin and use used for hunting deer and wild boar, this breed is descended from the last representatives of the Céris and the Montemboeuf which were direct descendants of the Chiens Blancs du Roy, the pack-hounds of the French King Louis XII in the fifteenth century. The breeder, G. Hublot du Rivault, gave them the name Billy which was that of his home in Poitou.

Appearance Head fine, lean, not too broad and not too long with a medium long skull, sufficiently broad muzzle, slight stop. **Eyes** rather large, dark, lively expression. **Ears** medium length, slightly folded, pendulous. **Neck** of moderate length, with little throatiness. **Body** moderately long with a very deep chest, flat ribs. **Legs** long, strongly-boned. **Feet** round. **Tail** long. **Coat** short and hard.

148 Bloodhound (Chien de Saint Hubert)

Origin and use the Bloodhound came to England in 1066 with William the Conqueror. According to legend, the Chien de Saint Hubert already hunted in the Belgian Ardennes with its forebears in the seventh century.

Appearance Head long, narrow, with ample skin falling in loose folds. The muzzle a little narrower than the skull, no stop. **Eyes** hazel to yellow, deeply sunken with haw. **Ears** thin, very long, hanging down in folds. **Neck** long, with much throatiness. **Body** short, with deep chest, well-sprung ribs. **Legs** moderately long. **Feet** strong and short. **Tail** long. **Coat** short.

Character shy, tolerant, affectionate, sensitive.

145

Height at withers: about 18–22 inches (45½–56 cm).
Colour: white with black patches and pale or dark tan markings.

147

Height at withers: dog: 24½–26½ inches (62–67 cm), bitch: 23–25 inches (58½–63½ cm).
Colour: self-coloured white; white with light coffee colour; white with orange or lemon patches or mantle.

148

Height at withers: dog: about 26½ inches (66 cm), bitch: about 24½ inches (61 cm).
Colour: black and tan, liver (red) and tan, solid red. Small white markings allowed except on the head.

149 Bracke, Deutsche

Origin and use many of the numerous old types of German hounds are almost or altogether extinct, but this one remains, and in 1955 the Deutscher Bracken Club established a standard for the breed.

Appearance Head long cast with a narrow skull, long muzzle which is a little narrower than the skull, little stop. A light stripe runs over the middle of the nose. **Eyes** brown and bright, with a friendly expression. **Ears** rather long, broad, hanging flat. **Neck** of moderate length, strong. **Body** moderately long, very deep chest, slightly-arched ribs. **Legs** long, thin and strong. **Feet** longer than cat-feet. **Tail** long. **Coat** medium short hair, hard, coarse and dense.

Character lively, friendly, affectionate.

150 Bracke, Oesterreichische Glatthaarige (Brandl Bracke, Austrian Hound)

Origin this breed is an old indigenous hound of the Austrian province of Karintia, descended from the Celtic hounds and akin to the Swiss Jura Hound and the Bloodhound.

Appearance Head with a broad skull, not too long muzzle, slight stop. **Eyes** brown and bright. **Ears** medium sized, pendant and flat. **Neck** of medium length, without throatiness. **Body** rather long, fairly broad with a very deep chest. **Legs** of medium length. **Feet** round. **Tail** long. **Coat** dense, smooth and glossy.

Character lively, kind, working breed.

151 Bracke, Steierische Rauhaarige Hochgebirgs (Peintiger Bracke, Styrian Rough-haired Mountain Hound)

Origin and use the breed comes from the Austrian province of Styria. In the last quarter of the nineteenth century, Hanoverian trail hounds, Karintian Hounds and rough-haired Istrian Hounds, were crossed to obtain a tough utility dog for hunting in the high mountains.

Appearance Head rather long, with a moderately broad skull, straight muzzle, slight stop. **Eyes** brown to yellow. **Ears** not too large drop ears. **Neck** of medium length. **Body** rather long with a deep chest. **Legs** of medium length. **Feet** oval. **Tail** long. **Coat** rough, lying close to the body.

Character active, faithful, strong hunting instinct, only suitable for hunting.

149

Height at withers:
18–21 inches
(45½–53½ cm).
Colour: red yellow,
yellow, grey, black.
Black mingled with
dark grey or yellow,
fawn or golden
brindle. White blaze,
collar, white on chest,
legs and tail tip.

150

Height at withers:
18–20 inches
(45½–51 cm).
Colour: black with tan
or yellow markings,
red, tan, red mingled
with black. White
patch on breast
allowed.

151

Height at withers:
16–20 inches
(40½–51 cm).
Colour: red and drab
yellow. White patch
on breast allowed.

152 Bracke, Tiroler (Tyrolese Hound)

Origin derived from the Austrian province of Tyrol and narrowly akin to the Brandlbracke.

Appearance Head long, rather narrow skull and muzzle, slight stop. **Eyes** brown. **Ears** moderately long, broad drop ears. **Neck** shorter than head, without throatiness. **Body** fairly long, more narrow than broad with a very deep chest, pronounced breast. **Legs** medium long, strongly-boned. **Feet** short. **Tail** long. **Coat** short or rough.

Character energetic, trustworthy, can be used as beater and tracker.

153 Briquet Griffon Vendéen

Origin and use a breed derived from the Grand Griffon Vendéen of which it is a smaller version.

Appearance Head with rounded, not too broad skull, broad muzzle, marked stop. **Eyes** large, dark with a lively expression. **Ears** supple, not too long, folded and pendulous. **Neck** long and without throatiness. **Body** rather short, fairly deep, not too broad chest. **Legs** of medium length, straight and strongly-boned. **Feet** not too large and strong. **Tail** long. **Coat** hard, not too long, sometimes shaggy, woolly undercoat.

Character self-willed, independent, terrific hunting instinct.

154 Chien d'Artois

Origin and use this descendant of the Chien de Saint Hubert originated in northern France. At the start of the present century packs of these hounds, used for hunting hare, were still quite numerous.

Appearance Head rather broad skull, broad, not too short muzzle, marked stop. **Eyes** large and melancholy, with a gentle expression. **Ears** somewhat thick, rather long and pendulous. **Neck** fairly long, strong with very little throatiness. **Body** of medium length, not too deep, broad chest. **Legs** moderately long, strongly-boned. **Feet** oval. **Tail** long. **Coat** short and dense.

Character intelligent, courageous, affectionate.

152

Height at withers:
large size: 16–19½
inches (40½–49½ cm),
small size: 12–15½
inches (30½–39 cm).
Colour: basic colour
black, red or reddish
yellow with white
blaze, collar, breast
patch and tail tip; or
tricolour: black with
red on legs, breast,
belly and head and
white markings.

153

Height at withers:
dog: 20–22 inches
(51–56 cm), bitch:
19–21 inches
(48½–53½ cm).
Colour: fawn, hare-
coloured, white and
orange, white and
grey, white and hare-
coloured or black and
white; tricolour
combining all these
colours.

154

Height at withers:
about 21–24 inches
(53½–61 cm).
Colour: tricolour:
white and black with
fawn, hare or
badger.

155 Chien Français Blanc et Noir

Origin and use an inventory was made in France in 1957 of the hounds in the still extant packs. Most of these hounds were crossings from old purely French hound breeds. They were classified anew into three breeds, of which the Chien Français Blanc et Noir proved to be sufficiently pure-bred to make it possible for a standard to be set up. The principal blood which these hounds carry is of the Gascon-Saintongeois breeds, with which that of the Levesque as well as other strains are mingled.
Appearance Head long cast, rather narrow skull, long muzzle, slight stop. **Eyes** dark, with an intelligent and confident expression. **Ears** moderately long, slightly spiral and pendulous. **Neck** rather long, strong with slight throatiness. **Body** not too short, deep, not too broad chest and moderately-sprung ribs. **Legs** long, strongly-boned. **Feet** more long than short. **Tail** long. **Coat** short and thick.
Character affectionate, friendly.

156 Chien Français Blanc et Orange

Origin and use this dog is the result of crossing old French breeds belonging to the Grands Chiens Courants.
Appearance not yet sufficiently purebred to allow a standard to be set up.

157 Chien Français Tricolore

Origin and use when the new inventory was made in 1957 this crossing of old French breeds of Grands Chiens Courants proved to be sufficiently purebred for a standard to be set up for the breed.
Appearance Head moderately broad and long, slight stop. **Eyes** large, brown with an intelligent expression. **Ears** very supple, pendulous, rather long and slightly folded. **Neck** long, a little throatiness. **Body** deep chest, sufficiently-sprung ribs. **Legs** long, strongly-boned. **Feet** short. **Tail** long. **Coat** short, rather fine.
Character willing, affectionate, friendly.

158 Coonhound

Origin and use in the first years of the seventeenth century Bloodhounds were imported into Virginia, England's first North American colony, to defend the colonists against the Red Indians. It was not until the second half of the eighteenth century that, with the help of the progeny of these Bloodhounds, dogs were bred especially for hunting raccoon and opossum on foot. Among the many types of hounds used for this purpose, the Coonhound is, so far, the only one to have been recognized by the American Kennel Club.
Appearance Head with long, moderately broad skull, long, broad, deep muzzle, slight stop. **Eyes** hazel to dark brown. **Ears** long, folded and pendulous. **Neck** rather long without too much throatiness. **Body** of medium length, deep chest and well-sprung ribs. **Legs** long and well-boned. **Feet** short and strong. **Tail** long. **Coat** short and dense.
Character lively, friendly, keen.

155
Height at withers:
dog: 26–29 inches
(66–73½ cm), bitch:
25–27 inches
(63½–68½ cm).
Colour: black and
white. Black mantle
or large patches and
specks. Red specks
only allowed on legs.
Pale red markings
above the eyes, on
the cheeks, under the
eyes, under the ears
and at root of the tail.

157
Height at withers:
dog: 25–28 inches
(63½–71 cm), bitch:
24–27 inches
(61–68½ cm).
Colour: tricolour:
black, white and tan.

158
Height at withers:
dog: 24–27 inches
(62½–68½ cm),
bitch: 23–25 inches
(58½–63½ cm).
Colour: black and tan.

159 Dachsbracke (Alpenländisch-Erzgebirgler Dachsbracke, Erz Mountain Dachsbracke)

Origin and use from the Bohemian-Styrian Erz Mountains, the breed came to Austria, where it is now a versatile hunting dog in Steiermark and Karinthia. The Dachsbracke is an independent breed, it is not the result of crossing a hound with a Dachshund.

Appearance Head with rather broad skull, fairly long and strong muzzle, little stop. **Eyes** round, brown with a fiery expression. **Ears** broad, rather long, flat and pendulous. **Neck** of medium length, without throatiness. **Body** long, deep chest, well-sprung ribs. **Legs** short and heavily-boned. **Feet** round. **Tail** of medium length. **Coat** short, coarse and hard.

Character intelligent, energetic, affectionate.

160 Dachsbracke (Westfälische Dachsbracke)

Origin and use now very rare, this breed originated in Westphalia, Germany, by crossing a German hound and a Dachshund to obtain a short-legged hound.

Appearance Head with narrow, rather long skull and muzzle with little stop. **Eyes** dark and almond-shaped. **Ears** broad drop ears of medium length. **Neck** moderately long, strong, with throatiness. **Body** of medium length, narrow and not too deep chest. **Legs** short, straight, heavily-boned. **Feet** short and strong. **Tail** long. **Coat** dense, longish, short on the head and the lower part of the legs.

Character intelligent, calm, obedient.

161 Dachshund, Kurzhaar (Short-haired Dachshund)

Origin and use the Bibarhunt, which by the fifth century was used for hunting otter and badger, is said to be one of the ancestors of the Dachshund. Scent hounds and German pointers were used to build up the breed. The short-haired variety is the original type and once crooked as well as straight-legged Dachshunds were known. They are particularly effective tracking wounded game and working as beaters. The Miniature and Kaninchen have been bred especially for underground work.

Appearance Head long and lean, narrow skull, long, fine muzzle, as little stop as possible. **Eyes** medium large, oval and dark reddish-brown to black-brown, wall eyes allowed but not desirable for grey or patched dogs. **Ears** rather long and hanging flat. **Neck** rather long and without throatiness. **Body** long with a very protuberant breast-bone, deep chest and well-sprung ribs. **Legs** short and strong. **Tail** long. **Coat** dense, short and glossy.

Character intelligent, happy, disobedient, self-willed, affectionate, good watch-dog.

162 Dachshund, Kurzhaar Zwerg (Miniature Short-haired Dachshund)

Appearance similar to that of 161. Chest measurement 12–14 inches (30½–35½ cm).

163 Dachshund, Kurzhaar Kaninchen

Appearance similar to that of 161. Chest measurement up to 12 inches (30½ cm).

159

Height at withers:
13½–17 inches
(34–43 cm).
Colour: deer-red,
black with brownish-
yellow markings. Red
mingled with black
and black mantle.

160

Height at withers:
12–14 inches
(30½–35½ cm).
Colour: all the colours
of the German hounds
with more or less
white.

161

Chest measurement:
immediately behind
the elbows, over 14
inches (35½ cm).
Colour: all colours
permissible.

164 Dachshund, Langhaar (Long-haired Dachshund)

Origin some authorities claim that the Long-haired Dachshund is as old a variety as the Smooth-haired but others suggest that it results from crossing the Short-haired with the Setter and the Cocker Spaniel.

Appearance similar to that of 161, except for the **coat** which is long, soft, smooth and glossy.

165 Dachshund, Langhaar Zwerg
(Long-haired Miniature Dachshund)

Appearance similar to that of 164. Chest measurement: as for Miniature.

166 Dachshund, Langhaar Kaninchen

Appearance similar to that of 164. Chest measurement: as for 163.

167 Dachshund, Rauhaar (Wire-haired Dachshund)

Origin bred by crossing the Smooth-haired with the Schnauzer and the Dandie Dinmont Terrier.

Appearance similar to that of 161, except for the **coat**, which is wiry, hard and lying close to the body, with woolly undercoat. Marked beard and eyebrows are desirable, the **ears** practically short-haired.

168 Dachshund, Rauhaar Zwerg (Miniature Wire-haired Dachshund)

Appearance similar to that of 167. Chest measurement: as for 162.

169 Dachshund, Rauhaar Kaninchen

Appearance similar to that of 167. Chest measurement: as for 163.

170 Drever

Origin and use originated shortly after 1900 from Westphalian Dachs-bracke imported from Germany; the breed has developed in Sweden into an independent one which was recognized in 1949 under the name Drever. It is used for hunting fox, hare and wild boar. It is now one of the most popular breeds in Sweden.

Appearance Head long cast with a broad skull, blunt muzzle, slight stop. **Eyes** dark brown. **Ears** broad, moderately long and hanging flat. **Neck** long with loose skin on the throat but without flews. **Body** long with strong, very deep chest and well-sprung ribs. **Legs** short and strongly-boned. **Feet** oval and strong. **Tail** long. **Coat** rather short, dense and lying close to the body. **Character** calm, tenacious, devoted, intelligent.

164

Chest measurement:
as for 161.
Colour: as for 161.

167

Chest measurement:
as for 161.
Colour: as for 161.

170

Height at withers:
dog: 13–16 inches
(33–40½ cm), bitch:
12–15 inches
(30½–38 cm).
Colour: white with
black, tan or black
and tan markings.
White blaze, collar,
tip of tail and feet
desirable.

147

171 Dunker (Norwegian Hound)

Origin and use bred about 1820 in Norway by crossing the Russian Harlequin Hound with other hounds. The breed bears the name of its originator. This dog is particularly suited to hare hunting.

Appearance Head with moderately long, rather broad skull, long and broad muzzle, not too marked stop. **Eyes** rather large and dark, wall eyes are allowed for harlequin dogs. **Ears** medium broad and hanging flat. **Neck** long and lean. **Body** not too long, with a deep chest and well-sprung ribs. **Legs** moderately long, strongly-boned. **Feet** oval and strong. **Tail** long. **Coat** short and dense.

Character self-confident, affectionate, trustworthy.

172 Elkhound (Grey)

Origin and use a very ancient Norwegian breed, used for hunting big game (especially the elk). This is a very hardy and strong dog which has to work in intense cold over difficult terrain.

Appearance Head with broad skull, rather long, broad muzzle which narrows without being pointed, marked stop. **Eyes** dark brown with fearless, friendly expression. **Ears** very mobile prick ears. **Neck** of medium length and strong. **Body** short, with a broad, deep chest and well-sprung ribs. **Legs** moderately long, strongly-boned. **Feet** oval and strong. **Tail** curled. **Coat** of medium length, profuse and hard, with a soft woolly undercoat.

Character independent, friendly, intelligent.

173 Elkhound (Black)

Appearance similar to that of the Grey Elkhound, except for the **coat**, which is less full, the **colour**, which is black and the **height at withers**, which is less.

174 Erdeliy Kopo (Transylvanian Hound, Hungarian Hound)

Origin and use old hunting breed of the kings and princes who hunted bears and wolves in the mountains of eastern Hungary.

Appearance Head lean and not too heavy, with a medium broad skull and muzzle, slight stop. **Eyes** oval and dark brown. **Ears** moderately long and broad hanging flat. **Neck** rather long. **Body** long, with a very deep chest and well-sprung ribs. **Legs** of medium length, strongly-boned. **Feet** short. **Tail** long. **Coat** short, coarse and dense.

Character intelligent, fearless, costing little to keep.

171

Height at withers:
19–22 inches
(48½–56 cm).
Colour: black or blue
marbled (harlequin)
with brown or white
markings.

172

Height at withers:
dog: 21 inches
(52 cm), bitch:
19 inches (47 cm).
Colour: grey in several
shades with black tips
to the hairs, lighter
colour on belly, legs,
breast and underside
of tail; undercoat
light coloured.

174

Height at withers:
dog: 20–24 inches
(51–61 cm), bitch:
somewhat smaller.
Colour: black, with
tan legs and markings
on the muzzle and
above the eyes.

175 Estonian Hound

Origin and use during the upheavals at the time of the Russian Revolution many Russian hound breeds were lost. The Estonian Hound is one of the three breeds of hounds which survive within the present territory of the USSR.

Appearance **Head** round skull and strong muzzle with little stop. **Eyes** dark brown. **Ears** long, folded and pendulous. **Neck** short and round. **Body** long, with a broad, deep chest and fairly round ribs. **Legs** rather short, strongly-boned. **Feet** oval. **Tail** long. **Coat** short, coarse and dense.

Character strong hunting instinct.

176 Finsk Spets (Finnish Spitz)

Origin and use it is assumed that the forebears of this ancient breed came to Finland with its first inhabitants. The Finnish Spitz is a close kin of the Russian Laiki. It is used for hunting birds and other game.

Appearance **Head** fox head, not too narrow skull, not too long, gradually tapering muzzle, marked stop. **Eyes** medium large, dark with a lively expression. **Ears** prick ears. **Neck** of medium length. **Body** almost square with a deep chest. **Legs** not too long. **Feet** round. **Tail** curled. **Coat** fairly long, standing off from the body, with a short, dense, soft undercoat and short on the head and foreside of the legs.

Character independent, sensitive, alert, lively, good watch-dog.

177 Finsk Stovare

Origin and use bred in Finland from English, German, Swiss and Scandinavian hounds; it is very popular there.

Appearance **Head** with moderately broad skull, long, non-tapering muzzle as long as the skull, slight stop. **Eyes** dark. **Ears** moderately long drop ears. **Neck** dry, medium long, not too heavy. **Body** of medium length with a long, deep chest. **Legs** moderately long. **Feet** short. **Tail** long. **Coat** short.

Character good-natured, gentle, affectionate, strong hunting instinct.

175
Height at withers:
about 20 inches
(51 cm).
Colour: black, with
white and yellow
markings.

176
Height at withers:
dog: 17½ inches
(44 cm), bitch: 15½
inches (39 cm).
Colour: chestnut red
or pale red-gold.
Paler colour or cream
on breast and feet
allowed.

177
Height at withers:
dog: 22–24½ inches
(56–62 cm), bitch:
21–23 inches
(53½–58½ cm).
Colour: yellow to
red-brown with black
saddle and white
markings on head,
neck, breast, feet
and tail tip.

178 Foxhound

Origin and use at the beginning of the seventeenth century, deer hunting, already very popular in France, also came into fashion in England. Specially selected horses and hounds were offered as presents by the French King Henri IV to King James I in 1603. These hounds, crossed with offspring from the white Chien de Saint Hubert, named Talbots, were the forebears of the Foxhound. This continued to be the most used hound for fox hunting, so popular in England. Unlike the Beagle, it is seldom a house dog.

Appearance Head with rather broad and long skull, fairly long and strong muzzle. Eyes brown. Ears of moderate length, broad and hanging flat. Neck long and lean. Body rather short, with deep chest and well-sprung ribs. Legs rather long and well-boned. Feet round. Tail long. Coat short, dense, hard and glossy.

Character energetic, friendly, affectionate, tolerant.

179 Gascogne, Grand Bleu de

Origin and use this is one of the few breeds remaining from the Grand Chiens Courants of the past. Henri IV of France owned a famous pack of these descendents of the Chien de Saint.Hubert.

Appearance Head rather strong and long cast, medium broad skull, long and strong muzzle, slight stop. Eyes dark chestnut-coloured with slight haw, somewhat sad, but gentle and trusting expression. Ears thin, long, folded and pendulous. Neck of medium length with much throatiness. Body rather long, deep, broad chest and moderately-sprung ribs. Legs long, strongly-boned. Feet long and oval like those of the wolf. Tail long. Coat not very short, harsh and dense.

Character calm, friendly, affectionate.

180 Gascon-Saintongeois, Grand

Origin and use in 1846 the first crossing took place between the last representatives of the Saintongeois and the robust Gascon to produce this breed which bears their ancient names. It is used for hunting roedeer.

Appearance Head lean, long cast skull and muzzle, slight stop. Eyes preferably dark chestnut. Ears fine, long, folded and pendulous. Neck of medium length, with little throatiness. Body long, with a deep chest. Legs long, strongly-boned. Feet oval. Tail long. Coat short and dense.

Character gentle, affectionate.

181 Gascon-Saintongeois, Petit

Origin and use a breed created smaller than the Grand specially for hare hunting.

Appearance similar to that of the Grand, except for the size. Height at withers: dog: $22\frac{1}{2}$–25 inches (57–$63\frac{1}{2}$ cm) bitch: 21–$23\frac{1}{2}$ inches ($53\frac{1}{2}$–$58\frac{1}{2}$ cm).

178

Height at withers:
about 23½ inches
(59½ cm).
Colour: tricolour:
white, black and
tan or bicolour:
white and lemon.

179

Height at withers:
dog: 25–28 inches
(63–70 cm), bitch:
24–26 inches
(60–65 cm).
Colour: white
speckled with black
and black patches.
Two black patches
encircle the eyes and
the ears and there is
often a small oval
black patch on the
skull. Red markings
above the eyes, on the
cheeks, the lips, the
inside of the ears
and the legs and
beneath the tail.

180

Height at withers:
dog: 25–28 inches
(63½–71 cm), bitch:
24–26 inches
(61–66 cm).
Colour: white with
black specks and
black mantle or
patches. Pale red
markings. On the
hindfeet above the
hock is a small grey-
brown spot called
'marque de chevreuil'.

182 Grahund

Origin and use out of the many very ancient Scandinavian hunting dogs belonging to the spitz and pole dog families, standards were set up for a few purebred types and among these the FCI recognized the Grahund as a Swedish-Norwegian breed.

Appearance Head broad skull, strong muzzle (which is a little shorter than the skull and tapers) and practically no stop. Eyes dark brown. Ears prick-ears. Neck of medium length and strong. Body short, with a deep, broad chest and well-sprung ribs. Legs medium long and strongly-boned. Feet small and rather long. Tail curled. Coat rather long, straight and hard, with a soft undercoat. It is shorter on the head and the front of the legs.

Character self-confident, energetic, friendly to familiar people.

183 Griffon Fauve de Bretagne

Origin and use in Brittany and elsewhere, this hound is used for hunting fox and wild boar. When it was on the brink of extinction, the breed was saved by the efforts of a few breeders who fostered it.

Appearance Head long cast, not too broad skull, rather long, not too narrow muzzle, slight stop. Eyes dark with a bold expression. Ears not too long, supple and pendulous. Neck rather short and muscular. Body short, broad and a deep chest with well-rounded ribs. Legs of medium length, strongly-boned. Feet strong. Tail long. Coat not too long and very hard.

Character fiery, enterprising.

184 Griffon Nivernais

Origin and use indigenous to the Nivernais district in central France, this old breed is especially used for hunting boar.

Appearance Head lean and light, with rather narrow skull, fairly long muzzle, slight stop. Eyes preferably dark, with a lively and piercing expression. Ears supple, half long, slightly folded and pendulous. Neck rather light and without throatiness. Body fairly long with a rather deep, not too broad chest. Legs rather long, fairly lightly boned. Feet oval. Tail long. Coat long, shaggy, tousled, coarse and hard.

Character courageous, affectionate, lively.

182

Height at withers:
dog: 21 inches
(53½ cm), bitch:
20 inches (49 cm).
Colour: different
shades of grey,
undercoat pale grey.

183

Height at withers:
dog: 20–22 inches
(51–56 cm), bitch:
19–21 inches
(48½–53½ cm).
Colour: fawn.

184

Height at withers:
20–24 inches
(51–61 cm).
Colour: preferably
wolf-grey or blue-
grey, wild boar grey or
drab black with tan
markings, or dark
fawn.

185 Hannoverischer Schweisshund

Origin and use in about 1800 sportsmen from Hanover crossed the heavy Solling-Leitbracke, akin to the Chien de Saint Hubert, with the lighter Haidbracke and a type of hound from the Harz, to obtain faster trackers.
Appearance Head broad skull, light folds of skin, strong muzzle, slight stop. **Eyes** bright and dark brown, with an earnest expression. **Ears** more than medium long, very broad and hanging flat. **Neck** long and heavy, with much throatiness. **Body** long with a broad, deep chest and well-sprung ribs. **Legs** rather short, straight or slightly crooked and heavily-boned. **Feet** round. **Tail** long. **Coat** dense, smooth and glossy.
Character calm, trustworthy, affectionate.

186 Harrier

Origin and use the Harrier is one of the most ancient English breeds. Some of today's packs date from the middle of the eighteenth century. Their forebears were French hounds which came to England with the Normans. French Basset blood was added and later on that of the Fox-hound, as a result of which they became less heavy. They are used for hunting hare and are seldom kept as house dogs. There is no recognized standard for the breed. The Masters of the several packs breed following their own judgement in selecting the type of hound most suited to the terrain in which they hunt.
Appearance Head longer and less deep than that of the Foxhound, with slight stop. **Eyes** brown with a friendly expression. **Ears** moderately long and hanging flat. **Neck** long, strong and without throatiness. **Body** rather short with deep chest and well-sprung ribs. **Legs** of moderate length and well-boned. **Feet** cat-feet. **Tail** long. **Coat** not too short and coarse, sometimes broken-haired.
Character lively, friendly, affectionate.

187 Hygenhund

Origin and use this dog was bred in the second half of the nineteenth century by the Norwegian breeder Hygen who crossed Holsteiner Hounds with other types of hounds.
Appearance Head with broad skull and rather pointed muzzle which gives the head a triangular appearance; slight stop. **Eyes** dark. **Ears** pendulous. **Neck** long and strong. **Body** moderately long, deep, rather broad chest and well-sprung ribs. **Legs** of medium length; strongly-boned. **Feet** strong and large. **Tail** long. **Coat** short, dense and hard.
Character trustworthy, affectionate.

185
Height at withers:
dog: 20–24 inches
(51–61 cm), bitch:
16–20 inches
(40½–51 cm).
Colour: grey brown,
red brown, all shades
of yellow, brown with
black brindle.

186
Height at withers:
about 18½–22 inches
(47–56 cm).
Colour: all hound
colours.

187
Height at withers:
about 22 inches
(56 cm).
Colour: yellow with
small or large white
markings.

188 Istrski Gonič Kratkodlaki (Short-haired Istrian Hound)

Origin and use this ancient Yugoslavian breed from Istria, is used for hunting hare and fox and as a tracker.

Appearance Head with long, moderately broad skull and muzzle, slight stop. Eyes round and as dark as possible. Ears thin, broad and hanging flat. Neck strong, without throatiness. Body rather long with a moderately broad, deep chest and slightly-sprung ribs. Legs fairly long and well-boned. Feet cat-feet. Tail long. Coat smooth, fine, dense and glossy.

Character keen, friendly, lively.

189 Istrski Gonič Resati (Wire-haired Istrian Hound)

Appearance Much the same as the short-haired type, except for the **coat** which is 2–4 inches (5–9 cm) long, rough, and stands off from the body, with a soft and dense undercoat. **Height at withers:** 18½–23 inches (45½–56 cm).

190 Jämthund

Origin and use this breed from Sweden is closely related to the Norwegian Elkhound but unlike that breed it is practically unknown outside its own country, where it is very popular. For many centuries Elk have been hunted in the forests of Sweden and Norway with these spitz-type hounds. Sportsmen of Jämtland county raised their own larger type which was recognized as an independent breed in 1946.

Appearance Head with broad skull, medium long, not too pointed muzzle, marked stop. Eyes dark brown. Ears large prick-ears. Neck strong and of medium length. Body short with a deep broad chest and strongly-arched ribs. Legs long and heavily-boned. Feet oval. Tail curled. Coat moderately long, hard and dense, with a short, soft undercoat. It is shorter on the head and the front of the legs.

Character self-assertive, affectionate, friendly, intelligent.

191 Jura Laufhund (Bruno)

Origin and use of the four Swiss hounds this one from the Jura mountains of Switzerland most closely resembles the Chien de Saint Hubert (see also the Berner Laufhund).

Appearance similar to that of the Berner except in colour.

192 Jura Laufhund (Saint Hubert)

Origin and use Bloodhounds were used when this breed was re-introduced and consequently it offers a fair copy of the Chien de Saint Hubert as shown on old pictures.

Appearance similar to that of the Bruno type, except for the **head** which is heavy, with a broad skull, long, broad muzzle, distinct stop and loose skin. **Neck** long and broad with throatiness. **Body** broad, deep chest. **Legs** strongly-boned.

188
Height at withers:
large size: 18–23
inches (45½–58½ cm),
small size: 16–18
inches (40½–45½ cm).
Colour: white with
orange-yellow
patches.

190
Height at withers:
dog: 23–25 inches
(58½–63½ cm), bitch:
21–23 inches
(53½–58½ cm).
Colour: dark to light
grey. Light grey or
cream on muzzle,
throat and underside
of tail.

191
Height at withers:
about 18–22 inches
(45½–56 cm).
Colour: solid yellow
or reddish brown or
these colours with
black saddle. Black
with yellow-red
markings. White
patch on breast
permissible.

193 Jura Niederlaufhund

Appearance similar to that of the large size except for the **height at withers** which is 12–15 inches (30½–38 cm).

194 Karelsk Bjornhund (Karelian Bear Dog)

Origin and use this stubborn and quarrelsome dog has been purebred in Karelia, Finland, since 1935, where attempts have been made to moderate its temperament. A relative of the Russian Laiki, the breed has been also used in that country for hunting bears, lynx and elk.
Appearance Head with fairly broad skull, wedge shaped muzzle, slight stop. **Eyes** rather small, dark brown with fiery expression. **Ears** prick ears. **Neck** of medium length, without throatiness. **Body** not too short with an ample, oval, deep chest. **Legs** moderately long. **Feet** roundish, with the hindfeet longer than forefeet. **Tail** curled. **Coat** straight with stiff upperhair and soft, dense undercoat.
Character pugnacious, intolerant, temperamental.

195 Levesque

Origin and use named after its breeder this dog carries chiefly Saintongeois and Gascon blood mixed with some English blood.
Appearance Head with broad skull, not too long, broad muzzle and marked stop. **Eyes** rather large, light chestnut brown, with a gentle and intelligent expression. **Ears** not too long, slightly folded and pendulous. **Neck** strong with little throatiness. **Body** long with a rather deep, broad chest. **Legs** long and strongly-boned. **Feet** round and strong. **Tail** long. **Coat** short and dense.
Character affectionate, friendly.

196 Lundehund

Origin and use this breed, which originated on the island Vaerög, has long been used in northern Norway for catching the puffin (*Lund* in Norwegian) and to search for eggs on the rocks and cliffs along the coast.
Appearance Head wedge shaped with a moderately broad skull, short and slightly hollow muzzle, marked stop. **Eyes** brown. **Ears** prick ears. **Neck** of medium length and strong. **Body** fairly long, with a deep chest. **Legs** not too short, strongly-boned, all have double dew claws. **Feet** strong. **Tail** curled. **Coat** fairly long and hard, lying close to the body, with a dense undercoat.
Character intelligent, lively, temperamental.

Height at withers:
dog: 21½–24 inches
(54½–61 cm), bitch:
19½–22 inches
(49½–56 cm).
Colour: brownish
black with white
markings.

Height at withers:
dog: 26–29 inches
(66–73½ cm), bitch:
25–27 inches
(63½–68½ cm).
Colour: white and
black with a large
mantle or small or
large specks; pale red
markings.

Height at withers:
9–10 inches
(23–25½ cm).
Colour: black, grey or
brown in different
shades, with white.

197 Luzerner Laufhund

Origin and use bears the name of the Swiss town of Lucerne, (see also the Berner Laufhund).

Appearance similar to that of the Berner, except for the shortness and colour of its coat.

198 Luzerner Niederlaufhund

Appearance similar to that of the large size except for the coat which can also be wire-haired and the height at withers 12–15 inches (30½–38 cm).

199 Ogar Polski (Polish Hound)

Origin and use this ancient breed of hunting dogs is very popular in its native Poland, but little known elsewhere.

Appearance Head moderately broad and long skull and muzzle, with slight stop. Eyes brown. Ears medium long and pendulous. Neck rather long, with a little throatiness. Body fairly long with a broad chest and slightly-rounded ribs. Legs of moderate length and well-boned. Feet short. Tail long. Coat smooth and dense.

Character affectionate, friendly.

200 Otterhound

Origin and use like the other English hounds, this old breed is descended from the Chien de Saint Hubert, crossed in this case with much Griffon blood, especially that of the Griffon Vendéen. In the course of time Harrier, English Water Spaniel and Bloodhound bloods were introduced and later still, in the last 150 years, crossing took place with the Kerry Beagle, the Staghound and the Foxhound. The first known pack of Otterhounds belonged to King John in 1212. This breed, exclusively used as a hunting dog, has no recognized standard. The Otterhound is a good swimmer, a necessary accomplishment in a dog used for hunting the otter.

Appearance Head heavy with not too broad skull, strong, deep muzzle, slight stop. Eyes brown with a slight haw. Ears long and hanging in a fold. Neck rather long and strong. Body not too long with a deep chest and well-sprung ribs. Legs moderately long, strongly-boned. Feet large and round. Tail long. Coat fairly long and very rough, with good hard hair and dense waterproof undercoat.

Character intelligent, faithful, independent.

197

Height at withers: about 18–22 inches (45½–56 cm). Colour: pale grey-black or black-white speckled with large black patches. Tan or yellow markings.

199

Height at withers: 20–24 inches (51–61 cm). Colour: black, with tan underside.

200

Height at withers: about 24–26 inches (61–66 cm). Colour: all hound colours.

201 Petit Bleu de Gascogne

Origin and use this descendant of the Grand Chien Bleu de Gascogne was bred for hare hunting.

Appearance Head rather long and light, with a long cast but not pointed muzzle, little stop. **Eyes** chestnut. **Ears** not too thin, long, slightly folded and pendulous. **Neck** fine and rather long, with little throatiness. **Legs** moderately long, strongly-boned. **Feet** rather long and oval. **Tail** long. **Coat** not too short and dense.

Character affectionate, calm, friendly.

202 Petit Griffon Bleu de Gascogne

Appearance it is very like the Petit Bleu de Gascogne except for its size and **coat** which is dry, rough, lies close to the body and should not be too long, and especially much shorter on the ears. **Height at withers:** 17–21 inches (43–53½ cm).

203 Poitevin

Origin and use in the eighteenth century several packs of hounds of various descent occurred in Poitou, in south-west France. In 1842 rabies caused the loss of the pack to which the forebears of the present Poitevin belonged except for one dog and two bitches. The breed, used particularly for hunting wolves, was built up again with the help of English blood.

Appearance Head large and not too broad, slight stop. **Eyes** large and brown. **Ears** thin, of medium length, slightly folded and pendulous. **Neck** long, fine, without throatiness. **Body** rather short, with a deep, not too broad chest. **Legs** long and strongly-boned. **Feet** oval and strong. **Tail** long. **Coat** short and glossy.

Character intelligent, lively.

204 Porcelaine (Chien de Franche-Comte)

Origin and use this very ancient French breed for hunting hare and roedeer has remained very pure. It is a close kin of the Swiss Schweizer Laufhund.

Appearance Head rather long and lean, broad skull, rather long, moderately broad muzzle, little stop. **Eyes** preferably dark. **Ears** fine, fairly long, well folded and pendulous. **Neck** rather long and light, may have some throatiness. **Body** long, not too fine. **Feet** longish and strong. **Tail** long. **Coat** short, fine, dense and glossy.

Character friendly, lively, affectionate.

201

Height at withers:
19–22½ inches
(48½–57½ cm).
Colour: blue or white
with black specks and
black patches; tan
markings.

203

Height at withers:
24–27½ inches
(61–70 cm).
Colour: tricolour:
white, red and black;
black mantle or large
patches. Bicolour:
white and red.

204

Height at withers:
dog: 22–23 inches
(56–58½ cm), bitch:
21–22½ inches
(53½–57½ cm).
Colour: snow white
with orange patches.
Orange specks on the
ears are very
characteristic.

205 Rhodesian Ridgeback

Origin and use these dogs have a characteristic 'ridge' on the back which comes from dogs the Hottentots brought from Asia to South Africa. The offspring of these dogs were crossed many times with hounds and mastiffs, but the ridge remained. A missionary took two of these dogs from the Cape to Rhodesia, where they proved to excel at hunting big game and even lions. For this reason it used to be called Lion Dog but the breed was profusely bred in Rhodesia and hence was given the name of that country.

Appearance Head lean with a broad skull, long, deep muzzle and reasonably marked stop. **Eyes** round, their colour must harmonize with that of the coat, with an intelligent expression. **Ears** medium-sized and pendulous. **Neck** long and strong. **Body** fairly long with a not too broad but deep chest and well-sprung ribs. **Legs** long and strongly-boned. **Feet** round and strong. **Tail** long. **Coat** short, dense, fine and glossy, with a ridge of hair along the spine which grows in the reverse direction to the rest of the coat beginning with two crowns behind the shoulder, equal to not more than one third of the ridge, which then tapers to a point above the haunches.

Character friendly, energetic, devoted, good watch-dog.

206 Russian Hound (Drab Yellow)

Origin and use indigenous Russian hounds were crossed with imported Foxhounds to produce this breed which was not recognized until 1925. In its own country it is the most popular hound.

Appearance Head with moderately broad and long skull and muzzle with little stop. **Eyes** round. **Ears** flat, pendulous and medium long. **Neck** broad. **Body** long with a deep chest and rounded ribs. **Legs** rather long and strongly-boned. **Feet** oval. **Tail** long. **Coat** short, dense and hard.

Character strong hunting instinct.

207 Russian Hound

Origin and use bred in Siberia and in the forests and steppes of European Russia for hunting hare, fox and sometimes badger.

Appearance Head with rather broad skull and muzzle, slight stop. **Eyes** dark. **Ears** small, triangular and pendulous. **Neck** short and round. **Body** long with a deep chest. **Legs** fairly long and strongly-boned. **Feet** oval. **Tail** long. **Coat** short, dense and hard.

Character strong hunting instinct.

205
Height at withers:
dog: 25½–27½ inches
(63½–68½ cm), bitch:
24½–26½ inches
(61–66 cm).
Colour: from light
wheaten to rich red.
Some white on toes
and breast allowed.

206
Height at withers:
dog: 23–26 inches
(58½–66 cm), bitch:
21½–25 inches
(54½–63½ cm).
Colour: black with
drab yellow.

207
Height at withers:
dog: 23–26 inches
(58½–66 cm), bitch:
21½–25 inches
(54½–63½ cm).
Colour: tan with or
without black saddle,
with white or yellow
markings.

208 Sabueso Español de Monte (Sabueso Hound large size)

Origin and use this very ancient breed is descended from the Celtic Hound and was named after the first inhabitants of central France. Originally only used in packs, it is now also used as a tracker by the police.
Appearance Head large with the skin much folded, a broad round skull, long, heavy and pointed muzzle, little stop. **Eyes** brown and deeply set. **Ears** large, long, folded and pendulous. **Neck** of medium length and very heavy, with throatiness. **Body** fairly long with broad, deep chest and well-sprung ribs. **Legs** rather short and strong. **Feet** round. **Tail** long. **Coat** short, hard and dense.
Character energetic, temperamental, self willed, persevering.

209 Sabueso Español Lebrero (Sabueso Hound small size)

Appearance very similar to that of the De Monte except that it is smaller and lighter in weight. In this variety the **colour** patches may almost cover the body except for the neck, muzzle, chest and feet.
Height at withers dog: should not exceed 20½ inches (52 cm), bitch: should not exceed 19½ inches (49½ cm).

210 Schweizer Laufhund

Origin and use see Berner Laufhund.
Appearance similar to that of the Berner, except for its **colour**.

211 Schweizer Niederlaufhund

Appearance similar to that of the large size except for the **height at withers** 12–15 inches (30½–38 cm).

212 Segugio Italiano a Pelo Raso e a Pelo Forte (Short- and Rough-haired)

Origin and use the only old hound breed of the Italian mainland, descending from the hound of the Celts. Used singly as a gundog as well as in a pack.
Appearance Head fine and long, with a fairly long, narrow skull and muzzle, slight stop. **Eyes** large and dark. **Ears** long, fine and pendulous. **Neck** long and lean. **Body** moderately long, with deep chest and slightly-sprung ribs. **Legs** long with strong, not too heavy bones. **Tail** long. **Coat** short: 1 inch (2½ cm), rough: 2 inches (5 cm); both of them hard, dense and lying close to the body.
Character persevering, affectionate, gentle.

208

Height at withers:
dog: 20½–22½ inches
(52½–57½ cm), bitch:
19½–21½ inches
(49½–54½ cm).
Colour: white with
large dark or light
orange or black
patches.

210

Height at withers:
18–22 inches
(45½–56 cm).
Colour: white with
large or small
yellow-red or deep red
patches. Red mantle
allowed. A few red
spots are not a fault.

212

Height at withers:
dog: 20–22½ inches
(51–57½ cm), bitch:
19 inches (48½ cm).
Colour: dull black or
reddish brown or
tricolour: black and
reddish brown with
white legs and
patches on neck and
feet.

213 Slovensky Kopov (Slovakian Hound)

Origin and use descended from the various hounds which have occurred from old in the Balkans.

Appearance Head moderately broad skull, medium-length muzzle, slight stop. **Eyes** dark. **Ears** medium-sized drop-ears. **Neck** not too long, without throatiness. **Body** long-cast with well-arched ribs. **Coat** of medium length, lying close to the body, thick undercoat.

Character affectionate, very gentle, strong hunting instinct.

214 Stövare, Halden

Origin and use named after the town of Halden in Norway, where it was developed from indigenous hounds and foxhounds.

Appearance Head medium long and broad skull and muzzle, marked stop. **Eyes** dark. **Ears** moderately long and hanging flat. **Neck** of moderate length and strong. **Body** moderately long, with a deep chest and well-sprung ribs. **Legs** moderately long, strongly-boned. **Feet** rather short. **Tail** long. **Coat** short and dense.

Character gentle, trustworthy, affectionate.

215 Stövare, Hamilton

Origin and use a breed named after the Swedish sportsman Hamilton created from the now extinct Holsteiner and Hanoverian Heidebracke crossed with the Curlandish Hound and the Foxhound. It is the most recent of the three Swedish Stövare breeds. These hounds do not hunt in a pack but work alone over the deep snow in the vast forests of their native land.

Appearance Head long, rather narrow skull, long and strong muzzle, little stop. **Eyes** dark brown. **Ears** fairly short and pendulous. **Neck** long without throatiness. **Body** long cast, with deep chest and well-sprung ribs. **Legs** long and strongly-boned. **Feet** strong. **Tail** long. **Coat** moderately short, dense and smooth.

Character friendly, devoted, lively.

213
Height at withers:
dog: 16–20 inches
(40½–51 cm), bitch:
16–18 inches
(40½–45½ cm).
Colour: black and tan.

214
Height at withers:
about 26 inches
(66 cm).
Colour: white with
black patches, brown
shadings on head and
legs and around the
patches.

215
Height at withers:
dog: 20–24 inches
(51–61 cm), bitch:
18½–22½ inches
(47½–57½ cm).
Colour: black with
brown markings on
head, legs, belly and
underside of tail.
White blaze and white
on neck, legs and feet.

171

216 Stövare, Schiller

Origin and use the forebears of this breed, which is named after its creator, came from south Germany, Austria and Switzerland. These dogs, which bred true much earlier than the Hamilton Stövare, are used for hunting snow-hare and fox and as trackers.

Appearance Head long, broad skull, long muzzle, marked stop. **Eyes** dark brown. **Ears** supple, of medium length and pendulous. **Neck** long and strong. **Body** rather short with deep chest and well-sprung ribs. **Legs** long and strongly-boned. **Feet** oval. **Coat** moderately short, dense and smooth; in winter there is a dense undercoat.

Character Friendly, happy, devoted.

217 Stövare, Småland

Origin and use the oldest of the three Stövare breeds, which originated in the dense forest country of Småland in southern Sweden. It is used for hunting fox and hare.

Appearance Head long, with rather broad skull, strong muzzle, marked stop. **Eyes** preferably dark. **Ears** of medium length and pendulous. **Neck** of medium length, without throatiness. **Body** short with deep chest and well-sprung ribs. **Legs** long and strong. **Feet** short. **Tail** long or congenitally short. **Coat** dense, coarse, smooth and glossy, with a dense, soft undercoat.

Character calm, friendly, devoted.

218 Alano

Origin and use this dog was produced in Spain by crossing the descendants of the Celtic hounds with mastiffs. As their hunting capacity surpasses their protecting instinct, they are considered to belong to the hunting dogs, in spite of their mastiff-like appearance. They are used in a pack for the pursuit of the wild boar and to hold it at bay.

Appearance Head massive with broad skull, heavy, short and square muzzle, deep stop. **Eyes** large, brown, slightly protruding with a courageous, somewhat malevolent expression. **Ears** moderately large and pendulous. **Neck** strong, rather long, with throatiness. **Body** rather short with broad, deep chest and round ribs. **Legs** rather short and strongly-boned. **Feet** round. **Tail** long. **Coat** short and rough. **Height at withers** about 23 inches (58½ cm). **Colour** red with black muzzle.

219 Thal-Tan Bear Dog

Origin and use this ancient breed is named after the Thal-tan Indians of Canada. Used for hunting bear, lynx and porcupine.

Appearance Head resembles that of the fox, with a moderately wide skull, pointed muzzle, marked stop. **Eyes** dark. **Ears** very large prick ears. **Neck** of medium length. **Body** rather short, deep chest. **Legs** long and strongly-boned. **Feet** oval and strong. **Tail** of moderate length, from 5–8 inches (13–20½ cm) and exceptionally thick from root to tip. **Coat** dense.

Character self-confident, bold, good-natured, affectionate.

216
Height at withers:
dog: 20–24 inches
(51–61 cm), bitch:
18½–23 inches
(47½–58½ cm).
Colour: black with
brown.

217
Height at withers:
dog: 18–21 inches
(45½–53½ cm), bitch:
17–20 inches
(43–51 cm).
Colour: black with
brown markings
above the eyes and
low on legs. Very
small white markings
on feet and tail.

219
Height at withers:
12–16 inches
(30½–40½ cm).
Colour: solid black
or blue-grey with
white spots or white
with black head and
black spots.

220 Argentinian Mastiff

Origin and use used for hunting puma and wild boar.
Appearance Head with rounded skull, rather short and broad muzzle, marked stop. **Eyes** dark with a lively, intelligent and sharp expression. **Ears** cropped. **Neck** strong, much throatiness. **Body** with deep, not too broad chest and well-sprung ribs. **Legs** rather long and strongly boned. **Feet** strong and short. **Tail** long. **Coat** short. **Height at withers** dog: 25–26 inches (63½–66 cm); bitch: 23–24 inches (58½–61 cm). **Colour** white.
Character courageous, pugnacious.

221 Balkanski Goniči

Origin and use a Yugoslavian breed, used for hunting fox and hare.
Appearance Head rather broad skull, moderately long muzzle, little stop. **Eyes** large and dark. **Ears** moderately long and broad, pendulous. **Neck** of medium length, without throatiness. **Body** long cast, with broad, deep chest. **Legs** rather long and well-boned. **Tail** long. **Coat** short, dense and thick. **Height at withers** 18–21 inches (45½–63½ cm). **Colour** deep red, brown with black saddle or mantle reaching to the head; black markings above the eyes.
Character docile, gentle, good-tempered, diligent.

222 Ellinitos Ichnilatis

Origin and use this hound is used in Greece over all kinds of terrain.
Appearance Head long with scarcely perceptible stop. **Eyes** brown with a lively, questioning expression. **Ears** moderately long, carried close to the head. **Body** long with rather broad, deep chest. **Tail** long. **Coat** short, dense and rough. **Height at withers** dog: 18½–21½ inches (47½–54½ cm), bitch: 17½–21 inches (44½–53½ cm). **Colour** black and tan.

223 Keltski Goniči

Origin and use this breed is found in Illyria, Yugoslavia.
Appearance Head rather long and broad skull; strong, square and blunt muzzle. **Eyes** round. **Ears** rather long and pendulous. **Neck** rather short, without throatiness. **Body** fairly short with deep, broad chest and well-sprung ribs. **Legs** of moderate length. **Tail** long. **Coat** 4 inches (9 cm) long, stiff, hard and standing off; undercoat short, soft and dense; ears short-haired. **Height at withers** about 11–22 inches (45½–56 cm). **Colour** whitish, wheaten, reddish, tan, drab grey.

224 Kerry Beagle

Origin and use probably a crossing of English and French hounds with the Bloodhound as it was two hundred years ago.

Appearance a more French type, owing to its longer and more supple ears, and less compact shape than most of the English hounds. **Coat** short. **Height at withers** 22—23 inches (56—58½ cm). **Colour** black and tan.

225 Posavski Goniči

Origin and use this hound comes from the region of Posavina along the river Sava in Yugoslavia.

Appearance Head with long, not broad, skull and muzzle, slight stop. **Eyes** round and dark. **Ears** moderately long and pendulous. **Neck** of medium length without throatiness. **Body** rather long and strongly boned. **Tail** long. **Coat** varies from short to wire-haired. **Height at withers** 19—23 inches (48½—58½ cm). **Colour** yellow with white markings on head, neck, breast, legs and tail.

226 Rastreador Brasileiro

Origin and use used in Brasil for hunting the Jaguar, this breed was created by crossing the Coonhound, American and English Foxhounds and some other American types of hound.

Appearance a strongly built, coarse Foxhound, with rather long, thin ears and long thick **tail**. **Coat** short and stiff.

227 Trailhound

Origin and use north-east England, now exclusively used for racing over a scent trail laid over the Lake District fells.

Appearance the Trailhound is smaller and lighter than the Foxhound used in the hills. **Head** resembling that of the Foxhound, with a somewhat more pointed muzzle and longer ears. **Neck** moderately long. **Body** long with deep breast and moderately arched ribs. **Legs** more lightly boned than those of the Foxhound. **Feet** longer than cat-feet. **Coat** short. **Height at withers** about 22—26 inches (56—66 cm). **Colour** all colours occur.

228 Afghan Hound

Origin and use probably the forebears of this very ancient breed were imported gamehounds and indigenous mountain hounds. While outside its native country the breed is very popular as a show dog, in Afghanistan it is still a highly valued working dog, and is also used for hunting (especially the gazelle), for herding and as a watch-dog.

Appearance Head with long, not too broad skull, long strong muzzle, little stop. **Eyes** almond-shaped and slant upwards. **Ears** pendulous. **Neck** long and strong. **Body** of medium length, with a deep chest and well-sprung ribs. **Legs** long and strongly boned. **Feet** very large and strong, with the hindfeet narrower than forefeet. **Tail** long with a ring at the tip. **Coat** long and fine, except on muzzle. Short hair is also allowed on back.

Character reserved, dignified, intelligent, independent.

229 Borzoi

Origin and use this ancient Russian breed has long been very popular in Russia and outside its native country. In the second half of the nineteenth century several types of Borzoi occurred, which no longer survive. The Perchino Hounds from the pack of Grand Duke Nicolaï Nikolaevitch were the most uniform and it is from them that the present Borzoi for the major part descends. Originally used for hunting fox and hare, the Borzoi was bred sturdier and stronger in the first half of the nineteenth century so that it could hunt wolf.

Appearance Head long with both skull and muzzle narrow, no visible stop. **Eyes** dark. **Ears** rose ears. **Neck** moderately long and lean. **Body** medium length with arched loins, uncommonly deep, rather narrow chest, ribs flat or very slightly arched. **Legs** long, narrow seen from the front, broad seen from the side. **Feet** hare-feet. **Tail** long. **Coat** long, wavy or with large curls, glossy, short on head, ears, front of legs.

Character cool, aloof, peaceful, distrustful of strangers, self-composed.

230 Cirneco dell'Etna (Sicilian Hound)

Origin and use this Sicilian breed closely resembles the prick-eared hounds depicted in old Egyptian reliefs. It is practically unknown outside its native island, where it has remained very pure. Since the Second World War it has been carefully developed by some enthusiasts. It is used for rabbit hunting.

Appearance Head narrow with long skull and preferably long, not too fine muzzle, scarcely any stop. **Eyes** ochre, amber or grey. **Ears** large, triangular prick ears. **Neck** long and strong. **Body** deep, narrow chest, slightly arched ribs, straight back. **Legs** long and lightly boned. **Feet** resembling cat-feet. **Tail** long. **Coat** medium long, lying close to the body; shorter on the head, ears and limbs.

Character lively, friendly.

228

Height at withers:
dog: 27–29 inches
(68½–73½ cm), bitch:
25–27 inches
(63½–68½ cm).
Colour: all colours.

229

Height at withers:
dog: average 30
inches (76 cm),
bitch: average
28½ inches
(72½ cm).
Colour: preferably
solid white or white
with yellow, orange,
red, brindle or grey
patches; or one of the
aforesaid colours
without white.

230

Height at withers:
dog: 18½–21 inches
(46½–53½ cm), bitch:
17–18½ inches
(43–46½ cm).
Colour: solid red in
several shades to
isabella and
sand coloured or red
with white markings;
solid white or white
with orange patches or
drab red mantle
permissible.

231 Deerhound

Origin and use one of the oldest breeds of the British Isles, its forebears may have been introduced by the Phoenicians, this hound was developed in the highlands of Scotland. In Perthshire cave paintings predating the Christian era show rough-haired hounds hunting wolves and deer. The earliest documentary evidence for the breed dates from the ninth century but firm evidence of its appearance dates from the eighteenth. The collapse of the clan system after the Jacobite rebellions and the introduction of firearms jeopardized their existence, but a few enthusiasts have kept the breed alive. Now, instead of hunting the game independently, their task is to pursue the game and to hold it at bay. Even today there are places in the mountains still called after hounds who died hunting.

Appearance Head long, moderately broad skull, pointed muzzle, no stop. **Eyes** dark with gentle expression at rest, keen when roused. **Ears** small, thin rose ears. **Neck** long and strong. **Body** long, well-arched loins, not too broad, deep chest. **Legs** long and strongly boned. **Feet** strong. **Tail** long. **Coat** hard, rough, 3–4 inches (7½–9 cm) long, much softer on head, breast and belly.

Character obedient, intelligent, dignified, gentle, faithful.

232 Galgo Español

Origin and use this breed has the same ancestry as the Pharaoh Hound. It is used for hunting on horseback.

Appearance Head long, narrow skull, long tapering muzzle, scarcely visible stop. **Eyes** large and dark. **Ears** small, half pendulous. **Neck** long and strong. **Body** with slightly arched loins, deep, broad chest and well-sprung ribs. **Legs** long and strong. **Feet** slightly longer than cat-feet. **Tail** long. **Coat** short and fine or rough.

Character temperamental, aloof.

233 Greyhound

Origin and use this is a very ancient breed, if not the most ancient of the hounds which the Celts took to England. As the 'gazehound' of earlier times it was used by mounted hunters. Today it is raced at greyhound tracks which are very popular in many countries.

Appearance Head long, rather broad skull, long, strong muzzle, slight stop. **Eyes** dark with an intelligent expression. **Ears** small, thin rose ears. **Neck** long and muscular. **Body** long, deep roomy chest, well-sprung ribs, slightly arched loins. **Legs** long and strongly boned. **Feet** moderately long. **Tail** long. **Coat** fine, lying close to the body.

Character gentle, affectionate, aloof with strangers.

231

Height at withers:
dog: at least 30 inches
(76 cm), bitch: at least
28 inches (71 cm).
Colour: dark blue-grey
or dark and light grey
or brindle or yellow or
ginger; white breast,
toes and tip of tail not
wanted but allowed.

232

Height at withers:
dog: 26 inches
(66 cm), bitch:
24 inches (61 cm).
Colour: cinnamon,
chestnut, red, black,
white and
combinations of these
colours.

233

Height at withers:
dog: 28–30 inches
(71–76 cm), bitch:
27–28 inches
(68½–71 cm).
Colour: black, white,
red, blue, fawn, drab
red, or brindle; with or
without white.

234 Irish Wolfhound

Origin and use long ago, hounds of this type were introduced into Greece by the Celts. The Romans knew the breed and used it in the arena. In Ireland, the Wolfhound was held in high esteem from the twelfth to the sixteenth century. As a result of the extinction of wolves and the export of great numbers of dogs, the breed became very scarce and in 1652 export was prohibited by law. Even so in the middle of the nineteenth century only a few specimens of the old stock survived. By crossbreeding with the Deerhound the breed was given new life. Later on crossbreeding took place on one occasion only with a Tibetan Wolfhound and once with a Great Dane. Originally the Irish Wolfhound hunted wolf, bear, stag and the very large Irish Elk.

Appearance Head long, not too broad skull, long, moderately pointed muzzle, almost no stop. **Eyes** dark. **Ears** small rose ears. **Neck** rather long and strong. **Body** long, very deep, broad chest and arched loins. **Legs** long and well-boned. **Feet** moderately large and round. **Tail** long. **Coat** rough, hard and shaggy.

Character friendly, obedient, good with children.

235 Magyar Agár (Hungarian Greyhound)

Origin and use when, in the ninth century, the nomadic Magyars invaded what is now modern Hungary, they brought with them large herds of cattle, sheep-herding dogs and hounds intended for hunting. These Asiatic hounds were probably crossed with the progeny of the Roman hounds already extant in the country. In the twentieth century a great deal of Greyhound blood was added in order to obtain faster and more graceful dogs, as a result of which the original type was lost. After the Second World War only a few examples of the breed remained. At present efforts are being made in Hungary to recover the original type. The breed is used particularly for hare hunting.

Appearance Head long, broad skull, long, strong muzzle, marked stop. **Eyes** dark. **Ears** thick rose ears. **Neck** rather long and strong. **Body** not too long, rather straight back, deep chest with well-sprung ribs. **Legs** long and strongly boned. **Feet** fairly long. **Tail** long. **Coat** short, dense, rough or smooth.

Character calm, affectionate, good watch-dog.

236 Pharaoh Hound

Origin and use although in the opinion of many people they belong to one and the same breed, the FCI recognizes the Pharaoh Hound as well as the Podenco Ibicenco. They and the Cirneco dell'Etna all have an appearance which strongly resembles the dogs depicted on Egyptian tombs. Without any question the three breeds are closely related. It is supposed that the Pharaoh Hound came to Gozo and Malta with the seafaring Phoenicians who traded with North Africa, Malta and Greece.

Appearance Head long skull, slightly longer, strong muzzle, slight stop. **Eyes** dark amber with a fiery, intelligent expression. **Ears** fine prick ears. **Neck** long, lean and strong. **Body** long cast, almost straight back, deep chest and well-sprung ribs. **Legs** long and strongly boned. **Feet** short and strong. **Tail** long. **Coat** fine, short and glossy.

Character friendly, happy, affectionate.

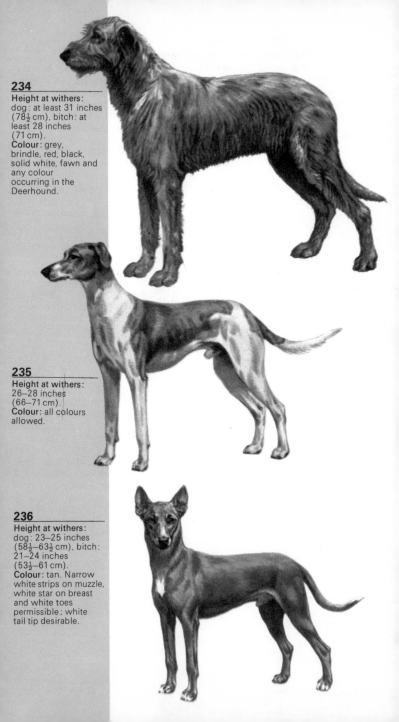

234
Height at withers:
dog: at least 31 inches
(78½ cm), bitch: at
least 28 inches
(71 cm).
Colour: grey,
brindle, red, black,
solid white, fawn and
any colour
occurring in the
Deerhound.

235
Height at withers:
26–28 inches
(66–71 cm).
Colour: all colours
allowed.

236
Height at withers:
dog: 23–25 inches
(58½–63½ cm), bitch:
21–24 inches
(53½–61 cm).
Colour: tan. Narrow
white strips on muzzle,
white star on breast
and white toes
permissible; white
tail tip desirable.

237 Podenco Ibicenco (Ibizan Hound)

Origin and use the Podenco Ibicenco is found on the isles of Ibiza, Formentera, Majorca and Minorca, and in the coastal districts of Catalonia. It is a very old breed and has the same ancestry as the Pharaoh Hound. They are used for hunting hare, rabbit and partridge, both as single dog or in a small pack, and are also said to retrieve.

Appearance Head long, narrow skull and muzzle, scarcely visible stop. **Eyes** bright amber to caramel, with an intelligent expression. **Ears** large prick ears. **Neck** sufficiently long and lean. **Body** with slightly arched loins, deep chest and flat ribs. **Legs** long and strong. **Feet** hare-feet. **Tail** long. **Coat** short or long.

Character happy, intelligent, good-natured, never aggressive.

238 Podenco Portugues

Origin and use the Portuguese Podenco is related to the Pharaoh Hound and the Podenco Ibicenco. There are three sizes which are used respectively for hunting larger game, hare or rabbit.

Appearance Head with moderately broad skull, rather short, slightly tapering muzzle, marked stop. **Eyes** small and brown. **Ears** large, thin, triangular prick ears. **Neck** long and lean. **Body** rather long, medium broad, deep chest and moderately arched ribs. **Legs** large size: rather long, medium size: rather short, small size: short. **Feet** round. **Tail** long. **Coat** short, smooth and soft or long, rough and without undercoat.

Character lively, intelligent, good watch-dog.

239 Saluki

Origin and use this is a Persian breed, but it probably originated in Arabia. It is related to the Afghan Hound and like that breed, in its own country occurs in many varied types which came into existence as a result of differences of terrain and the use made of them by diverse tribes. They are used for hunting many kinds of game, including hare, jackal and gazelle.

Appearance Head long and narrow, tapering towards the nose, moderately broad skull, long, strong muzzle and scarcely visible stop. **Eyes** large and dark to light brown, with a dignified and gentle expression, which when attentive becomes fiery and interested. **Neck** long. **Body** long cast, straight back, flat but very deep chest and very slightly arched ribs. **Legs** long with good bones. **Feet** rather long. **Tail** long. **Coat** soft, glossy, longer on ears, legs and tail, or without feathering.

Character intelligent, gentle, dignified, trustworthy with children, good watch-dog.

237
Height at withers:
dog: 26 inches
(66 cm), bitch:
24 inches (61 cm).
Colour: white with
red, white with lion
colour or solid white,
red or lion colour.

238
Height at withers:
large size: 22–28
inches (56–71 cm),
medium size: 20–22
inches (51–56 cm),
small size: 8–12
inches (20½–30½ cm).
Colour: yellow, fawn
or black grey; self-
coloured, multi-
coloured or patched.

239
Height at withers:
dog: 23–28 inches
(58½–71 cm), bitch: at
least 22 inches
(56 cm).
Colour: all colours
save solid white, solid
black and brindle.

240 Sloughi

Origin and use originally a dog of the Asiatic steppes, after the conquest of North Africa by the Arabs the Sloughi spread over the whole of the area north of the Sahara. At first the FCI considered it a French breed, but this hound has recently been recognized as Moroccan.

Appearance Head with flat skull as long as the wedge-shaped muzzle, scarcely a stop. **Eyes** large and dark, melancholy expression. **Ears** not too large, triangular and pendulous. **Neck** of medium length. **Body** of moderate length, long, not too broad, deep chest and well-sprung ribs. **Legs** long and lean. **Feet** a long cast and oval. **Tail** long. **Coat** smooth and fine.

Character affectionate to his master, aloof with strangers, calm, good watch-dog.

241 Tasy

Origin and use this Russian greyhound comes from central Asia and is also called the Mid-Asiatic Hound. The breed is unknown outside Russia, where it is used for hunting hare, fox, wildcat and wolf.

Appearance Head long and conical, not too narrow in skull and muzzle, no distinct stop. **Eyes** oval and large. **Ears** rose ears. **Neck** rather short and heavy. **Body** with slightly arched loins, very deep chest and well-sprung ribs. **Legs** long and strongly boned. **Tail** long. **Coat** short, dense and hard.

Character independent.

242 Whippet

Origin and use the origin is not clear. On the one hand crossbreeding between greyhound and terrier in the nineteenth century is supposed, on the other hand it is said that the Pharaoh Hound which probably came to England at the time of the Roman Conquest in 55 BC is one of his forebears. Considering its great likeness to the greyhound the first supposition seems the most probable. Originally used by English miners at rabbit catching matches and by poachers it was later, and is still, used for racing in Europe and in the United States.

Appearance Head with long skull and muzzle, slight stop. **Eyes** bright with lively expression. **Ears** thin rose ears. **Neck** long and well muscled. **Body** moderately long, very deep chest and well-sprung ribs, markedly arched loins. **Legs** long and strong. **Feet** short and strong. **Tail** long **Coat** fine, short and dense.

Character affectionate, courageous, good with children.

240
Height at withers:
22–30 inches
(56–76 cm).
Colour: sandy or all
shades of fawn with or
without black mask.
Drab white, brindle or
black with tan
markings on head,
feet and sometimes
on breast.

241
Height at withers:
dog: 24–27 inches
(61–68½ cm), bitch:
21½–26 inches
(54½–66 cm).
Colour: bright yellow,
yellow, drab grey,
black, grey yellow
and black with
yellow markings.

242
Height at withers:
dog: 18½ inches
(47 cm), bitch:
17½ inches (44½ cm).
Colour: any colour or
combination of
colours.

185

243 Chortaj (European-Russian Steppe Hound)

Origin and use from the many types of hounds occurring in Russia, four were selected at the Cynological Congress held at Moscow in 1952, as pure to be bred from in future. The Chortaj had earlier often been crossed with the Tasy. A passionate hunting hound, exclusively kept for that purpose, it is unknown outside its native country.

Appearance Head long, broad skull, strong tapering muzzle, slight stop. **Eyes** large. **Ears** thin, long rose ears. **Body** with arched loins and deep chest. **Legs** long, not heavy but strongly boned. **Tail** long. **Coat** fairly short and hard. **Colour** many colours allowed. **Height at withers** dog: 26 inches (66 cm), bitch: 25 inches (63½ cm).

244 South Russian Steppe Hound

Origin and use very similar to that of the Chortaj except for the **ears** triangular drop ears. **Coat** short and hard. **Height at withers** dog: 25–28 inches (63½–71 cm), bitch: 24–27 inches (61–68½ cm).

Gundogs

The gundog group evolved from the hounds. As early as the sixth century BC the Greek historian Xenophon mentions hounds which when approaching game did not pursue it but, sniffing the scent with raised head and quivering with excitement, stood completely still. Originally this was thought very undesirable behaviour in a sporting dog, but later it was realized that this quality could be put to use and such dogs were trained to help hunters in netting partridge and quail and for hawking. These dogs could easily be taught to crouch or lie down when they had scented the bird, the net then being drawn over both; or to put up the bird cautiously, which was then killed by the hawk.

They were originally called bird dogs, as the way in which they worked was suitable only for feathered game. Although gundogs are nowadays also used on fur (hare and rabbit) they are still used mainly for hunting birds. After the invention and development of firearms the bird dogs evolved into gundogs. First the dog searches out and finds his game by its body scent. It then indicates the location of the game to the sportsman by standing in full view pointing towards the quarry. On command he puts the game up and then retrieves it when it has been shot.

To produce a dog of this kind the hound's hunting drive had to be restrained and obedience bred. This must have been achieved by crossing hounds which showed an aptitude for finding their game by scent with head held high, with sheep-herding dogs, which are naturally obedient.

Hounds hunt according to inborn qualities and need little or no training, but for gundogs, however good their natural qualities, training for and support during their work is a must. Every dog is a hunter at heart and therefore a gundog which is to become a shooting dog needs supervision from an early age. He would instinctively enjoy chasing game but must not be given the chance to do so. If he once gets into that habit it will be difficult to cure and he will be spoilt for work with the gun.

In this group British Spaniels, French Èpagneuls and German Wachtelhund stand between the hound and the setters and pointers. They work at close range, that is to say, within range of the gun. When finding its game the dog should drop or remain steady until the game has been shot and then retrieve it. In covert or very rough country these dogs are sometimes expected to give tongue so that their owner knows where they are.

The Continental gundog is a versatile dog, for the owner expects its help in all aspects of shooting. British sportsmen, however, have made specialists of their gundogs as they consider the performance suffers if one makes a dog do diverse work. Their pointers and setters quarter the ground at high speed and stand steady when they have found game by scenting it. Retrievers sit quietly beside the gun, mark the game when shot and retrieve it on command. When game is only wounded they track it down and bring it to their handler.

As field trials became more popular, the dogs had to become faster. It is partly for this reason that in many breeds there is a wide divergence in type between the show and the working dog. The first corresponds to the standard as laid down when starting to breed pure dogs and describing the ideal working dog. In many breeds, however, the dogs now used for work deviate from the standard in appearance, because the sportsman, paying little attention to the dog's looks, has selected on the excellence of his working qualities and has chosen smaller and lighter dogs, which are faster. The show breeder keeps to the standard and usually has little interest in working qualities.

The best breeder for a working dog is one who strives to attain the dual-purpose dog. He does not choose the easy road, but it will give him great satisfaction to have eventually built up a strain of good-looking workers. In many breed societies a great deal of attention is paid to keeping the working abilities alive. Some breeds of Continental gundogs are only owned by shooting men. The breeders insist that their dogs only go where they will be worked. With some reason they fear the special working qualities attained by so much care and trouble, will be lose if ignorant people start breeding.

A gundog is friendly, active, faithful and, when well-trained, an obedient companion. It is highly valued by many people for its many attractive qualities.

Scale of Gundog illustrations 1 :15

245 Barbet

Origin and use many long- and rough-coated breeds are descended from the Barbets. This very ancient French breed is supposed to be the ancestor of the Poodle, the Bichon and the Briard. About the middle of the present century, the breed was nearly extinct, only a few representatives remaining in the possession of older sportsmen. Since 1970 Barbets closely resembling the description of the breed as given in the sixteenth century have again appeared at shows. The Barbet is used for hunting water game.

Appearance Head round, with broad skull, short, square muzzle and distinct stop. **Eyes** round and dark brown. **Ears** long, thick, hanging flat. **Neck** heavy and rather short. **Body** with broad, not too deep chest and well-sprung ribs. **Legs** rather short and well-boned. **Feet** large and round. **Tail** long. **Coat** woolly, long, thick and wavy, with a tendency to felt; or falling in cords.

Character temperamental, intelligent, fond of water, affectionate, courageous, untiring.

246 Bracco Italiano

Origin and use the old indigenous hounds of Italy were crossed with gundogs to bring this breed into being as early as the eighteenth century. It has altered very little since then. The Bracco Italiano on the one hand is less temperamental than the gundog and on the other less independent than the hound. The breed is little known outside its native country.

Appearance Head long and angular, rather broad, long skull, equally long, broad muzzle, slight stop. **Eyes** yellow to brown. **Ears** rather long and pendulous. **Neck** rather short and strong. **Body** with broad, deep chest and well-sprung ribs. **Legs** rather long and strongly boned. **Tail** docked $2\frac{1}{2}$–4 inches (6–10 cm). **Coat** short, dense and glossy.

Character calm, friendly, docile.

247 Braque de l'Ariège (Ariégeois)

Origin and use the province of Ariège, on the French-Spanish frontier is the home of this French breed, which descends from the Briquet and the Gascon-Saintongeois. It is used for hunting hare, and sometimes for larger game.

Appearance Head with narrow skull, long square muzzle, very slight stop. **Eyes** large with friendly expression. **Ears** fine, long, folded and pendulous. **Neck** long, with slight throatiness. **Body** long, broad and deep chest. **Legs** rather long and strongly boned. **Feet** strong. **Tail** docked. **Coat** short, fine and dense.

Character calm, somewhat stubborn, intelligent.

245

Height at withers:
18–22 inches
(45½–56 cm).
Colour: grey, black,
pale coffee, drab
white, white and
chestnut, white and
black.

246

Height at withers:
22–26½ inches
(56–67 cm).
Colour: white; white
with orange or amber
or white, speckled
with one of these
colours.

247

Height at withers:
dog: 22–24 inches
(56–61 cm), bitch:
21–23 inches
(53½–58½ cm).
Colour: white with
orange or chestnut
brown patches;
sometimes only
specks.

248 Braque d'Auvergne (Auvergne Pointer)

Origin and use this French gundog comes from Auvergne, in the south of France. It is said to be a descendant of the blue dogs brought by the Maltese Knights and was later crossed with pointers from Wales. The breed excels at hunting partridge and as retrievers.

Appearance Head with long, not too broad skull, long, square muzzle, distinct stop. **Eyes** dark hazel. **Ears** moderately long and pendulous, slightly folded. **Neck** long and rather heavy, with slight throatiness. **Body** with moderately broad, deep chest and well-sprung ribs. **Legs** rather long and well-boned. **Feet** between hare- and cat-feet. **Tail** docked to 6 inches (15 cm). **Coat** short, not too fine and glossy.

Character intelligent, docile.

249 Braque Français (French Pointer)

Origin and use this breed is undoubtedly the oldest of all gundog breeds. It has spread from the Pyrenees over large parts of the Continent with the result that the Braque Français became the progenitor of many, if not all Continental and British gundogs. It is closely related to the Spanish Gundog, which is also very ancient.

Appearance Head not too heavy, rather broad and long skull and muzzle, fairly deep flews, little stop. **Eyes** dark brown. **Ears** of medium length, slightly folded and pendulous. **Neck** sufficiently long, with slight throatiness. **Body** long, broad and deep chest, not exaggeratedly rounded ribs. **Legs** moderately long with good bones. **Feet** strong. **Tail** usually docked. **Coat** short, rough and dense.

Character intelligent, attentive, not pugnacious, good with children.

250 Braque Français Petite Taille

Appearance this dog differs from the previous breed in the following points. **Head** shorter muzzle. **Ears** shorter and hanging flat. **Neck** with less or no throatiness. **Height at withers** 19½–22 inches (49½–56 cm). **Colour** the brown colour is more extensive, often to a mantle, or one solid colour. The brown may be very light to very dark.

251 Braque Saint-Germain

Origin and use this breed was created in about 1830 by crossing old French gundogs with a pointer. The first cross took place at Compiègne near Paris. About twenty years later many of these dogs turned up at Saint-Germain-en-Laye, hence the breed's name. It is used for hunting larger game.

Appearance Head with a rather broad skull, long, fairly deep muzzle, distinct stop. **Eyes** golden, with good-natured expression. **Ears** rather short, thin, standing slightly off the head, pendulous. **Neck** rather long, some throatiness allowed. **Body** rather short with broad, deep chest and well-sprung ribs. **Legs** moderately long and strongly boned. **Feet** long. **Tail** long. **Coat** short, not too thin and never hard.

Character willing, gentle, aloof.

248

Height at withers:
dog: 23–25 inches
(58½–63½ cm), bitch:
22–24 inches
(56–61 cm).
Colour: white with
black patches and
fairly numerous
speckles; or a
charcoal grey
appearance created by
a few white hairs
mingled with
predominantly black.
The head should then
have regular black
markings, so that both
eyes are embedded in
the black.

249
Height at withers:
22½–26 inches
(57–66 cm).
Colour: white with
chestnut brown
specks and patches.

251
Height at withers:
dog: 22½–24½ inches
(57–62 cm), bitch:
21½–23½ inches
(54–59 cm).
Colour: dull white
with bright orange
patches. Some
speckling allowed
but not wanted.

252 Deutscher Wachtelhund

Origin and use in 1897, with the aim of producing a distinct type of working gundog, German breeders selected breeding stock strictly for the availability of the necessary working qualities in the long-haired working dogs which were the remaining descendants of the bird dogs of the eighteenth century. In this way the versatile Wachtelhund which gives tongue and is adapted to hunting in thick woodland originated. The Germans say 'it should only be in sportsmen's hands'.
Appearance Head lean, skull and muzzle of almost equal length and both rather broad. **Eyes** large, in all shades of brown. **Ears** hanging flat. **Neck** of medium length. **Body** not too short, deep, broad chest and slightly arched ribs. **Legs** rather short and strongly boned. **Feet** fairly large and somewhat long. **Tail** long. **Coat** long, glossy, slightly wavy, short on head. **Character** passionate, intelligent, obedient.

253 Drentse Patrijshond

Origin and use representatives of this Dutch breed, which originated in the province of Drente, appear in pictures painted several centuries ago. The breed has altered little or not at all in outward appearance. It is a useful working gundog for hunting many kinds of game on limited terrain.
Appearance Head with rather broad skull, broad wedge-shaped, blunt muzzle and shallow stop. **Eyes** amber, with good-natured, intelligent expression. **Ears** moderately large, hanging flat. **Neck** of medium length, without throatiness. **Body** not too short, rather broad, deep chest and well-sprung ribs. **Legs** moderately long and well-boned. **Feet** round to oval. **Tail** long. **Coat** not too long on the body, dense, straight, lying close to the body and well-feathered.
Character affectionate, gentle, docile, good with children, good watchdog.

254 Épagneul Breton

Origin and use this spaniel breed has occurred in Brittany for centuries. It is the only French spaniel which is also very popular outside its native country, especially in the United States. This multipurpose dog is suitable for working in water as well as on land.
Appearance Head with not too narrow skull of medium length and somewhat shorter muzzle, tight lips and distinct stop. **Eyes** dark amber with lively expression. **Ears** rather short and pendulous. **Neck** of medium length without throatiness. **Body** rather large and very deep chest with well-sprung ribs. **Legs** moderately long and strongly boned. **Feet** oval. **Tail** docked to 4 inches (10 cm) or congenitally tailless. **Coat** preferably smooth or slightly wavy, with slight feathering.
Character courageous, intelligent, lively, very affectionate.

252

Height at withers:
16–20 inches
(40½–51 cm).
Colour: brown, often
with white markings
on breast and legs;
white with large
brown patches and
specks; brown roan,
red roan, roan with
red or yellow
markings.

253

Height at withers:
22–25 inches
(56–63½ cm).
Colour: white with
large brown or orange
patches, tan markings
allowed; with or
without specks;
mantle allowed but
not desirable.

254

Height at withers:
18–20 inches
(45½–51 cm).
Colour: white and
orange, white and
chestnut; since 1933
also white and black.

255 Épagneul Français

Origin and use this old breed was very popular in the seventeenth and eighteenth centuries but in the nineteenth it was threatened with extinction. After a revival it was supplanted before the Second World War by English breeds and by the Épagneul Breton. It has reestablished itself since then and is now much appreciated in France as a working dog. Especially suited for work on differing terrain, the Épagneul Français is also an exceedingly good retriever.
Appearance Head with broad skull, long, broad muzzle and distinct stop. **Eyes** brown or dark yellow. **Ears** rather long, hanging flat. **Neck** rather short. **Body** long with broad, deep chest and flat ribs. **Legs** rather short and strongly boned. **Feet** large and round. **Tail** long. **Coat** profuse, smooth or slightly wavy, feathered on legs, ears and tail.
Character intelligent, obedient, willing, affectionate.

256 Épagneul Picard

Origin and use this is a very old and popular breed from Picardy in the north of France, and is particularly suitable for hunting in woods and marshes.
Appearance Head with broad, round skull, long, strong muzzle and flowing stop. **Eyes** dark amber, very expressive. **Ears** rather long and broad, pendulous. **Neck** of medium length. **Body** of medium length, deep, fairly broad chest. **Legs** not too long, strongly boned. **Feet** large and round. **Tail** long. **Coat** rough and slightly wavy, fine on the head, feathered on ears legs and tail.
Character intelligent, obedient, faithful.

257 Épagneul Bleu de Picardie

Appearance has many similarities to the Picard except that the **head** has an oval skull; light throatiness on the **neck** and the ribs are arched.
Height at withers 23–24 inches (58½–61 cm). **Colour** black-grey with small bluish, glossy patches; tan on head and legs allowed.

258 Épagneul Pont-Audemer

Origin and use opinions about the origin of this breed differ widely, but it is certain that crossing took place between one of the French Épagneuls and other breeds. Some authorities mention the Irish Water Spaniel, others speak of more than one crossing. The breed originated in the second half of the eighteenth century and at the beginning of the present century it was often seen in the neighbourhood of Pont-Audemer in Normandy. It is now rather scarce, This Épagneul excels at hunting woodcock, snipe and wild duck in deep water and marshland.
Appearance Head rounded skull, long, not too heavy muzzle, slight stop. **Eyes** small, chestnut brown to dark amber. **Ears** rather large and hanging flat. **Neck** moderately long and lean. **Body** with broad, deep chest and well-sprung ribs. **Legs** rather short and well-boned. **Feet** large and round. **Tail** docked to one third. **Coat** not too hard, curly hair which on ears and skull encircles a very short-haired face.
Character energetic, intelligent, faithful.

255

Height at withers:
22–25 inches
(56–63½ cm).
Colour: white with
chestnut-red patches
and sometimes
speckles.

256

Height at withers:
dog: 22–25 inches
(56–62 cm), bitch:
22–24 inches
(55–60 cm).
Colour: grey speckled
with chestnut-brown
patches; often with
tan on head and legs.

258

Height at withers:
21–23 inches
(53½–58½ cm).
Colour: chestnut
and grey or solid
chestnut or chestnut
with white.

259 Gamal Dansk Honsehund (Old Danish Pointer)

Origin and use this gundog came from Spain to Denmark in the seventeenth century. Great care was given to the revival of this very ancient breed and it was recognized by the Danish Kennel Club in 1962. It is a rather heavy dog suited to hunting in the flat Danish countryside.

Appearance Head deep and short with broad skull and muzzle, slight stop. **Eyes** of medium size, light to dark brown, with some haw. **Ears** long and broad, pendulous. **Neck** heavy with throatiness. **Body** rather short, broad, deep chest and well-sprung ribs. **Legs** rather short and well-boned. **Feet** short. **Tail** long. **Coat** short, dense and soft.

Character calm, attentive.

260 Griffon à Poil Dur (Korthals, Wire-haired Pointing Griffon)

Origin and use for many centuries rough-haired gundogs have appeared all over Europe which probably originated from the crossing of hunting dogs and rough-haired sheep-herding dogs which must have spread from Asia. In the second half of the nineteenth century the Dutchman, Korthals, created the Wire-haired Griffon which bears his name, out of the best of the dogs, which he found mainly in France, Germany and the Netherlands. The present representatives of the breed all go back to the eight ancestors used by Korthals. This Griffon is a very versatile gundog.

Appearance Head large and long, with not too broad skull, long, square muzzle, little stop. **Eyes** large, brown, with an intelligent expression. **Ears** medium sized, hanging flat. **Neck** rather long, without throatiness. **Body** with deep chest and slightly sprung ribs. **Legs** moderately long and strongly boned. **Feet** round and strong. **Tail** docked a good third. **Coat** not too long, rough, hard, with dense, soft undercoat.

Character intelligent, affectionate, obedient.

261 Griffon à Poil Laineux (Boulet, Long-coated Pointing Griffon)

Origin and use Emmanuel Boulet originated this breed in the north of France at the beginning of the nineteenth century. It is related to the Barbet and the Griffon Korthals and comes between those two breeds. It is a very useful gundog on varied terrains.

Appearance Head with medium sized skull and square, long and broad muzzle, **Eyes** yellow. **Ears** slightly folded and pendulous. **Neck** moderately long. **Body** not too short, fairly broad, deep chest. **Legs** moderately long and strongly boned. **Feet** short and strong. **Tail** docked. **Coat** soft, long, silky but not glossy, flat or slightly wavy.

Character intelligent, gentle, obedient.

259

Height at withers:
dog: about 22 inches
(56 cm), bitch: about
20½ inches (52 cm).
Colour: white with
light to dark brown
patches.

260

Height at withers:
dog: about 22–24
inches (56–61 cm),
bitch: about 20–22
inches (51–56 cm).
Colour: grey,
preferably blue grey or
grey with large brown
patches; or solid
brown, often mingled
with grey hairs; or
white with brown.

261

Height at withers:
dog: 21½–24 inches
(55–61 cm), bitch:
20–22 inches
(51–56 cm).
Colour: dull chestnut
brown to dead foliage
mingled with a few
white hairs with or
without small patches.

262 Münsterländer, Kleiner (Heidewachtel)

Origin and use at the beginning of the present century the Kleiner Münsterländer was bred in Westphalia in Germany out of old types of small, long-haired gundogs. It is related to the French Épagneuls and the Drentse Patrijshond and is a versatile working gundog.

Appearance Head with not too broad skull, long and strong muzzle, little stop. **Eyes** dark brown. **Ears** not too long, hanging flat. **Neck** of medium length. **Body** not too short, with deep chest and slightly arched ribs. **Legs** moderately long with not too strong bones. **Feet** round. **Tail** long. **Coat** long, lank, somewhat wavy, lying close to the body, slightly feathered.

Character intelligent, affectionate, obedient, good watch-dog.

263 Münsterländer, Grosser

Origin and use after the First World War the Grosser Münsterländer was developed by German sportsmen from the same stock they had used to create the Kleiner Münsterländer ten years before. Like all German gundogs, this is a spirited and versatile working dog.

Appearance Head long with moderately broad skull and muzzle and slight stop. **Eyes** dark. **Ears** hanging flat. **Neck** moderately long, strong and without throatiness. **Body** not too short, with deep, broad chest and slightly arched ribs. **Legs** of medium length and strongly boned. **Feet** between cat- and hare-feet and strong. **Tail** long. **Coat** long, smooth slightly wavy, short on head and well-feathered.

Character intelligent, affectionate, good watch-dog, ratter.

264 Perdiguero de Burgos (Perdiguero Burgales, Spanish Pointer)

Origin and use one of the most ancient Spanish breeds and in its own country a highly valued gundog on various terrains and used for hunting all kinds of small game.

Appearance Head with broad skull, square muzzle and slight stop. **Eyes** dark, with sad expression. **Ears** large, long, hanging in a fold. **Neck** sound, strong, with slight throatiness. **Body** long, deep, broad chest and rounded ribs. **Legs** long with heavy bones. **Feet** oval. **Tail** docked to two thirds. **Coat** short and smooth.

Character trustworthy, active, docile.

262
Height at withers:
dog: 20–22 inches
(51–56 cm), bitch:
19–21½ inches
(48½–54 cm).
Colour: brown with
white; brown roan;
tan markings on
muzzle and above the
eyes allowed.

263
Height at withers:
about 23–25 inches
(58½–63½ cm).
Colour: white with
black head, large black
patches on body and
irregularly distributed
smaller black patches
and black hairs in the
white.

264
Height at withers:
dog: 26–30 inches
(66–76 cm), bitch:
somewhat less.
Colour: white with
liver roan and liver
patches; liver with
grey-white roan.

265 Pordigueiro Portuguès (Portuguese Perdigeiro)

Origin and use this Portuguese partridge dog (*perdigueiro* means partridge) is probably related to the Spanish gundogs. The breed is unknown outside its own country but there it is a very popular working and house dog.

Appearance Head square seen from the front, rectangular from the side, broad skull, long, broad muzzle, very deep stop. **Eyes** dark hazel or brown. **Ears** large, thin and pendulous. **Neck** rather long, slight throatiness. **Body** short, rather broad, deep chest and well-sprung ribs. **Legs** rather long with good bones. **Tail** docked to two thirds. **Coat** short, rough and dense.

Character active, friendly, affectionate, obedient.

266 Pointer

Origin and use the blood of this highly valued and renowned swift working gundog has been successfully added to many breeds in order to make them more active, swifter and less clumsy. The Pointer itself, probably descended from the Spanish Pointer which is related to the French gundogs, was originally heavy and slow like that breed. After the shotgun had come into use English breeders succeeded in giving the Pointer his present-day shape. The breed's speciality is hunting feathered game; it has an excellent nose and is a staunch pointer. Crossings with the Foxhound, which took place to give the breed more stamina and constitution is the subject of controversy. It has undoubtedly impaired the typical head.

Appearance Head with moderately broad skull, which falls away beneath the eyes, equally long muzzle with concave nose bridge and distinct stop. **Eyes** hazel or brown, with friendly expression and downward glance. **Ears** of medium length and hanging supple. **Neck** long, round, strong and without throatiness. **Body** short, with moderately broad, rather deep chest and well-sprung ribs. **Legs** moderately long and strongly boned. **Feet** oval. **Tail** long. **Coat** fine, short, hard and glossy.

Character intelligent, lively, affectionate, gentle.

267 Pudelpointer (Poodle Pointer)

Origin and use about the end of the nineteenth century German sportsmen wanted to create a dog which would preserve the excellent qualities of the Pointer, a specialist in swift hunting and steady pointing, but be a more versatile breed, with a rough, dense coat for protection against cold, water and bushes. In the pursuit of this ideal, they crossed the Pointer with the very intelligent and fiery Poodle, descendant of the Barbet, which was originally a water dog and a retriever. Although the way proved to be a long and difficult one, the goal was reached at last. The Pudelpointers nowadays play an important role at field trials. Only dogs which have run a field trial with success are inscribed in the stud book.

Appearance Head with moderately long, broad skull, long, broad muzzle and deep stop. **Eyes** round, yellow to yellow brown, with hawkish expression. **Ears** lying flat. **Neck** of medium length and lean. **Body** not too short with moderately broad, deep chest and well-sprung ribs. **Legs** moderately long and strongly boned. **Feet** round. **Tail** docked. **Coat** of medium length, dense and wire-haired.

Character intelligent, lively, willing to learn.

265
Height at withers:
dog: about 22½ inches
(57 cm), bitch: about
21 inches (53½ cm).
Colour: usually red-
yellow to cream with
darker mask and ears.
Also allowed: solid
chestnut, white,
black, or patches of
one of these colours
on white background.

266
Height at withers:
dog: 25–27 inches
(63½–68½ cm), bitch:
24–26 inches
(61–66 cm).
Colour: the colours
which occur most are
yellow and white,
orange and white,
liver and white,
black and white,
solid colours and
tricolour also allowed.

267
Height at withers:
24–26 inches
(61–66 cm).
Colour: brown or the
colour of dead leaves.

268 Retriever, Chesapeake Bay

Origin and use it is said that when in 1807, a British ship was lost off the coast of Maryland, two dogs, Newfoundlands or Labradors, were saved with the crew. From crossings of these dogs with indigenous dogs, Retrievers and Otterhounds, came this retriever which was later called after Chesapeake Bay, where it was much in use. It is almost exclusively kept as a working dog and is nowadays increasingly seen outside its own country.

Appearance Head moderately long with broad skull, short, moderately broad muzzle and moderate stop. **Eyes** amber. **Ears** small, hanging flat. **Neck** of medium length. **Body** of medium length with broad, deep chest and well-sprung ribs. **Legs** of medium length and strongly boned. **Feet** large hare-feet. **Tail** long. **Coat** not longer than 1 to 1½ inches (2½–4 cm), thick, oily, fine with a woolly undercoat.

Character hard, stubborn, pugnacious, intelligent.

269 Retriever, Curly-coated

Origin and use the origins of this breed are uncertain. It is generally assumed that the Water Spaniel, the Poodle, the small Newfoundland dog, the forerunner of the present-day Newfoundland, and perhaps of one or two setter breeds, have played a part in its development. It is a good hunting dog, especially for water work.

Appearance Head long, with moderately broad skull, long, not pointed muzzle, practically no stop. **Eyes** black or brown. **Ears** rather small and pendulous. **Neck** moderately long. **Body** short with not too broad, deep chest and well-sprung ribs. **Legs** moderately long and strongly boned. **Feet** round. **Tail** long. **Coat** dense, short curls all over except on the face and skull.

Character intelligent, obedient, friendly, good watch-dog.

270 Retriever, Flat-coated

Origin and use it is supposed that the small Newfoundland, the large spaniels, setters and pointers are at the origin of this breed. The wavy-coated Retriever was developed first and became the ancestor of the present-day Flat-coated, the change in coat probably being due to the Collie. As the Flat-coated is a good retriever, the breed was very popular in England before the First World War. Later it was ousted by the Labrador and the Golden Retriever. Nowadays there is a growing interest in the Flat-coated both in and outside its native country.

Appearance Head long, medium broad skull, long, broad muzzle and little stop. **Eyes** dark brown or hazel with intelligent expression. **Ears** small, hanging flat. **Neck** long, without throatiness. **Body** rather broad, deep chest and well-sprung ribs. **Legs** moderately long and strongly boned. **Feet** round. **Tail** long. **Coat** of medium length, dense, lying close to the body.

Character intelligent, lively, obedient, good watch-dog.

268

Height at withers:
dog: 23–26 inches
(58½–66 cm), bitch:
21–24 inches
(53½–61 cm).
Colour: any colour
from faded brown to
dark brown or the
colour of dead grass,
from red brown to dull
straw yellow.

269

Height at withers:
25–27 inches
(63½–68½ cm).
Colour: black or liver.

270

Weight: 60–70 lb
(27–31½ kg).
Colour: black or liver.

271 Retriever, Golden

Origin and use the heavier black Wavy-coated Retriever sometimes produced a few yellow pups and it is believed that the Golden Retriever originated from the crossbreeding of these yellow retrievers with an old type of Water Spaniel and later with an Irish Setter, a Bloodhound and some black retrievers. In many countries the Goldens are now much sought after as working and show dogs.

Appearance Head with broad skull, broad, not too long muzzle, marked stop. **Eyes** dark. **Ears** moderately large and hanging flat. **Neck** rather long. **Body** short, deep chest and well-sprung ribs. **Legs** moderately long, with heavy bones. **Feet** round. **Tail** long. **Coat** long, smooth or wavy and well-feathered, with a dense undercoat.

Character intelligent, gentle, friendly, willing.

272 Retriever, Labrador

Origin and use it is generally assumed that the Labrador originated in Newfoundland. Its forebears are said to be black water dogs which used to swim between boats and the shore carrying things. It is not clear why the dogs were called Labradors. The third Earl of Malmesbury, who continued breeding this strain of water dogs from Newfoundland, used the name. The original dogs are practically extinct in Newfoundland, but the Labrador is a widely spread breed and, in England as well as elsewhere, the most popular of the retriever breeds as a working dog. It is also used as a guide dog for the blind and is a popular show and house dog. In later years retrievers, setters and pointers are said to have contributed to the improvement of the breed.

Appearance Head with broad skull, broad, medium long muzzle and slight stop. **Eyes** brown or hazel, with intelligent and good-natured expression. **Ears** hanging flat. **Neck** long and strong. **Body** short with broad, deep chest and well-sprung ribs. **Legs** moderately long and strongly boned. **Feet** round. **Tail** long and thick. **Coat** short, thick and hard.

Character trustworthy, obedient, good-tempered, good with children.

273 Setter, English

Origin and use one of the oldest gundog breeds, the setter originated in the seventeenth century from the spaniel and it is possible that the Spanish Pointer was also involved in its creation. In the nineteenth century two breeders, Edward Laverack and R Purcell Llewellin, developed the breed. Laverack bred a practically pure stock of English Setters which became very popular but were very self-willed. Llewellin crossed Laverack dogs first with Irish Setters and then with Gordon Setters. From these crossings a stock originated which was more suitable for hunting. The present-day show dogs descend from this stock. There is now a striking difference in type between the working and the show dogs.

Appearance Head long, with moderately broad skull, rather broad, moderately deep almost square muzzle; the skull and muzzle are of equal length, distinct stop. **Eyes** dark hazel. **Ears** moderately long, hanging with a fold. **Neck** rather long, without throatiness. **Body** of medium length, deep chest, well-rounded ribs. **Legs** moderately long and heavily boned. **Feet** short and strong. **Tail** long. **Coat** wavy, long, silky, short on head and well-feathered.

Character gentle, affectionate, calm.

271

Height at withers:
dog: 22–24 inches
(56–61 cm), bitch:
20–22 inches
(51–56 cm).
Colour: any shade of
gold or cream.

272

Height at withers:
dog: 22–22½ inches
(56–57 cm), bitch:
21½–22 inches
(54½–56 cm).
Colour: solid black,
yellow or chocolate.

273

Height at withers:
dog: 25½–27 inches
(64½–68½ cm), bitch:
24–25½ inches
(61–64½ cm).
Colour: black and
white; dark or light
orange and white;
black, white and tan;
liver and white. The
colours may be very
small to larger patches.

274 Setter, Gordon

Origin and use the first stock of these Scottish setters which originated about 1770 at Gordon Castle was lost through the sale of the kennel. About 1835, when he came to the Gordon title, the Duke of Richmond and Gordon revived the breed, but it is not known how he did this. There is mention of a Collie bitch, the Bloodhound and the Irish Setter. The Gordon Setter is the heaviest of the three setter breeds and is also the least swift.

Appearance Head more deep than broad, moderately broad skull, long, rather broad, almost square ended muzzle, distinct stop. **Eyes** dark brown. **Ears** fairly long, thin and pendulous. **Neck** long, without throatiness. **Body** rather short, deep, not too broad chest and well-rounded ribs. **Legs** moderately long and heavily boned. **Feet** oval. **Tail** long. **Coat** long, soft, glossy, straight or slightly wavy, shorter on head and well-feathered.

Character strong personality, affectionate, happy.

275 Setter, Irish

Origin and use the Irish Setter has certainly been bred purely in Ireland, where hunting was a popular sport. Little is known about the origin of the breed. At first this setter was red and white and only a single solid red one occurred here and there. It is impossible to retrace the means by which the pure red setter was obtained. The red colour is now the only recognized one, but the red and white dogs are still used by Irish sportsmen and bred by them as an independent breed.

Appearance Head long, rather narrow skull, long, fairly deep, almost square ended muzzle, distinct stop. **Eyes** dark, hazel or dark brown. **Ears** of medium length, fine and hanging with a fold. **Neck** of medium length, not too thick, without throatiness. **Body** in proportion, deep chest, rather narrow in front and well-sprung ribs. **Legs** fairly long and strongly boned. **Feet** small and strong. **Tail** long. **Coat** long, smooth, glossy; short on head and front of legs and well-feathered.

Character temperamental, affectionate, gentle.

276 Spaniel, American Cocker

Origin and use between the two World Wars the English Cocker Spaniels bred in the United States began to differ so much in type from the dogs in England that it became impossible to judge them as belonging to one and the same breed. So, in 1945, the breeds were separated and each was officially recognized with its own standard. In the United States, in order to be inscribed in the stud book, a dog had to carry pure English Cocker Spaniel blood for three generations. Thus there has been no crossing in the United States, whereas in England crossing took place with various other Spaniel types and with the Irish Setter in order to obtain several improvements which in the United States were only achieved by selective breeding.

Appearance Head rather short, broad skull, short, broad, deep and square muzzle and marked stop. **Eyes** dark brown to black, dark hazel or hazel, according to the colour of the coat, with intelligent, beseeching expression. **Ears** lobe-shaped, long, hanging flat. **Neck** long and lean. **Body** square, with deep, rather broad chest and well-sprung ribs. **Legs** moderately short and strongly boned. **Feet** round. **Tail** docked. **Coat** medium long, flat or slightly wavy, silky, well-feathered and short on head.

Character happy, lively, proud, curious.

274
Height at withers:
dog: 26 inches
(66 cm), bitch:
24½ inches (62 cm).
Colour: black with
tan markings.

275
Height at withers:
about 26 inches
(65 cm).
Colour: rich chestnut.

276
Height at withers:
dog: 14½–15½ inches
(36½–39 cm), bitch:
13½–14½ inches
(34½–36½ cm).
Colour: solid black or
other colours;
particoloured, roan,
black and tan.

277 Spaniel, American Water

Origin and use sportsmen in the United States have bred the American Water Spaniel by crossing imported Irish Water Spaniels and Curly-coated Retrievers. It is used in marshy country for hunting watergame and also rabbits.

Appearance Head of medium length with broad skull and muzzle, slight stop. **Eyes** hazel or brown. **Ears** long, hanging flat. **Neck** round, of medium length and without throatiness. **Body** long, deep, moderately broad chest and well-sprung ribs. **Legs** moderately short and strongly boned. **Feet** compact. **Tail** long. **Coat** dense, fine and curled.

Character lively, friendly, affectionate.

278 Spaniel, Clumber

Origin and use the origin of this dog, which is the oldest among the well known spaniel breeds, is not clear. It certainly came to England from the Continent and it is assumed that the Duc de Noailles started the breed in the eighteenth century by crossing a now extinct type of spaniel and a Basset At the approach of the French Revolution he took his dogs to the safety of the Duke of Newcastle's seat at Clumber Park but perished after his return to France. The famous kennel remained in England and since then has borne the name of the estate where it had found shelter. The present-day Clumbers still entirely conform with the dogs represented in the oldest pictures of the breed. They are highly valued as retrievers and for putting up game.

Appearance Head large with moderately broad skull, deep, moderately long, broad muzzle and deep stop. **Eyes** dark amber. **Ears** vine leaf shaped and pendulous. **Neck** rather long and thick. **Body** heavy deep, broad chest and strongly arched ribs. **Legs** short and heavily boned. **Feet** large and round. **Tail** docked. **Coat** long, profuse, dense, silky and smooth, the legs well-feathered.

Character calm, dignified, willing.

279 Spaniel, Cocker

Origin and use undoubtedly one of the oldest English spaniel breeds, about the origin of which little is known. The breed was not recognized by the Kennel Club until the end of the last century, after which more uniformity was obtained. Although the Cockers are very good and versatile gundogs, they are now bred and kept all over the world as show and house dogs. Nevertheless, in England, kennels of Cocker Spaniel exist which specialize in working dogs.

Appearance Head not too broad nor too long skull, square muzzle, distinct stop. **Eyes** hazel or brown, with intelligent and gentle expression. **Ears** lobe-shaped, thin, long and pendulous. **Neck** long and strong. **Body** short, with deep, not too broad chest and well-sprung ribs. **Legs** rather short and strongly boned. **Feet** cat-feet. **Tail** docked. **Coat** long, smooth, silky, feathered, short on muzzle and face.

Character happy, gentle, affectionate.

277

Height at withers:
15–18½ inches
(38–46½ cm).
Colour: liver or dark
chocolate; white on
toes and breast
permissible.

278

Weight: dog: 55–70 lb
(25–32 kg), bitch:
45–60 lb (20–27 kg).
Colour: white with
light lemon patches;
orange allowed but
not desirable. Slight
markings on head and
speckled fore-muzzle
with white body
preferred.

279

Height at withers:
dog: about 15½–16
inches (39–40½ cm),
bitch: about 15–15½
inches (38½–39 cm).
Colour: many colours,
solid as well as
multicoloured.

280 Spaniel, English Springer

Origin and use with the exception of the Clumber Spaniel, all spaniel breeds find their origin in the English Springer Spaniel, whose oldest stud book goes back to 1813. A very famous field trial dog was born from this stock in 1903, Velox Powder, who won twenty trials. Many trial and show dogs who reached the top were descended from this stock.

Appearance Head medium long, rather broad skull, rather broad, deep muzzle, distinct stop. **Eyes** dark hazel with friendly and lively expression. **Ears** lobe-shaped, fairly long, hanging flat. **Neck** rather long, without throatiness. **Body** with moderately broad, deep chest and well-sprung ribs. **Legs** not too short and strongly boned. **Feet** round. **Tail** docked. **Coat** long, dense, soft, feathered and soft on face and muzzle.

Character active, happy, affectionate, good with children.

281 Spaniel, Field

Origin and use before the Kennel Club recognized the several types of spaniels as distinct breeds at the end of the last century, they were not purely bred. The sportsman chose the type of spaniel most appropriate to the game and the country he shot over. The types occurring in a litter were called by different names and these became the names of the breeds. In order to obtain a spaniel which would more easily get under brushwood than the Springer Spaniel and would be less active than the Cocker, these latter two were crossed with each other and with the Sussex Spaniel. The lower and longer dog resulting from this combination became the Field Spaniel.

Appearance Head moderately broad and long skull, long, not too broad muzzle, distinct stop. **Eyes** dark hazel, brown, or nearly black. **Ears** of medium length, hanging folded. **Neck** long and strong. **Body** of medium length, not too broad, deep chest and well-sprung ribs. **Legs** not too short with strong, not too heavy bones. **Feet** round. **Tail** docked. **Coat** long, straight or slightly wavy, dense, silky, well-feathered and short on muzzle and face.

Character intelligent, affectionate, obedient.

282 Spaniel, Irish Water

Origin and use little can be said for certain about the origin of this spaniel. The supposition that the breed originated from a crossing of a Poodle and an Irish Setter can be discarded because of the totally different structure of the coat. The absolutely true breeding of the Irish Water Spaniel indicates that it has been bred for a long time without infusion of foreign blood.

Appearance Head comparatively broad, long skull, long, strong, somewhat square muzzle, distinct stop. **Eyes** amber, with intelligent expression. **Ears** very long, lobe-shaped and pendulous. **Neck** rather long and strong. **Body** short, deep, not too broad chest and well-sprung ribs. **Legs** rather long and strongly boned. **Feet** large and round. **Tail** long. **Coat** stiff curls, short on face and muzzle, and on the tail 3 inches ($7\frac{1}{2}$ cm) from the root.

Character intelligent, affectionate, courageous.

280

Height at withers:
dog: about 20 inches
(51 cm), bitch:
somewhat less.
Colour: preferably
liver and white; black
and white; these
colours with tan
markings. All land
spaniel colours are
allowed, except red
and white.

281

Height at withers:
dog: about 18 inches
(45½ cm), bitch:
somewhat smaller.
Colour: solid black,
liver, golden liver,
mahogany or roan;
one of these colours
with tan markings.

282

Height at withers:
dog: about 21–23
inches (53½–58½ cm),
bitch: about 20–22
inches (51–56 cm).
Colour: dark liver
with purplish lustre.

283 Spaniel, Sussex

Origin and use this breed originated at Rosehill Park in Sussex and has been known for a hundred years. In 1954, in order to infuse fresh blood, a cross was made with the Clumber Spaniel and produced good results. Originally used exclusively as a gundog, the Sussex later appeared at shows. It is scarce outside England and even there, together with the Field Spaniel, is the least known spaniel breed. It tends to hunt giving tongue, which is generally accepted.

Appearance Head medium long, broad skull, rather long, square muzzle, distinct stop. **Eyes** deep amber to hazel, with gentle, languishing expression. **Ears** thick, rather large, lobe-shaped and hanging flat. **Neck** moderately long and strong. **Body** fairly long, deep rather broad chest and well-sprung ribs. **Legs** rather short and heavily boned. **Feet** large and round. **Tail** docked to 5–7 inches (13–18 cm). **Coat** long, profuse, lying close to the body, well-feathered, short on face and muzzle.

Character one-man dog, lively, docile.

284 Spaniel, Welsh Springer

Origin and use this breed, which is frequently found in the Neath Valley, was clearly originally related to the Épagneul Breton, and may have been introduced to Wales by Gauls from Brittany. Until recently it was used mainly for hunting, but it appears with increasing frequency at shows in and outside its native country.

Appearance Head moderately long, broad skull, medium long, broad, rather square muzzle, distinct stop. **Eyes** hazel or dark brown. **Ears** rather small, hanging flat. **Neck** long, strong and without throatiness. **Body** not long, deep, not too broad chest and well-sprung ribs. **Legs** of medium length with good bones. **Feet** compact. **Tail** docked to two thirds. **Coat** long, dense, flat, silky, well-feathered, short on face and muzzle.

Character obedient, active, friendly.

285 Spinone

Origin and use this long established Italian breed originated in France in the district of Bresse and from there spread to Piedmont in north Italy. The Barbet, the Porcelaine and the French Griffon are mentioned among its forebears. Later crossings with the Griffon Korthals and the Drahthaariger Deutscher Vorstehund were not successful as far as the outward appearance was concerned, but improved the hunting capacities. Italian sportsmen like to use the Spinone in marshy country and in woodland.

Appearance Head long, rather narrow skull, equally long, square muzzle, slight stop. **Eyes** dark yellow to ochre. **Ears** triangular, hanging flat. **Neck** rather short with throatiness. **Body** short, deep, rather broad chest and well-sprung ribs. **Legs** long and strongly boned. **Feet** strong. **Tail** docked to 6–10 inches (15–25½ cm). **Coat** hard, dense, shaggy, 1½–2½ inches (4–6 cm) long, shorter on head, ears and foreside of legs; dense undercoat.

Character trustworthy, affectionate, docile.

283

Height at withers:
15–16 inches
(38–40½ cm).
Colour: liver brown
with gold lustre.

284

Height at withers:
about 18–19 inches
(45½–48½ cm).
Colour: dark red
with white.

285

Height at withers:
dog: 24–26 inches
(61–66 cm), bitch:
22–24 inches
(56–61 cm).
Colour: white; white
with orange or
chestnut patches
and spots.

286 Stabyhoun

Origin and use this dog, which originated in the Dutch province of Friesland, was at first a versatile working dog for rough shooting. It is presumably related to the Drentse Patrijshond and the Heidewachtel.

Appearance Head moderately broad, fairly long skull, equally long, strong muzzle and slight stop. Eyes dark brown for the black particoloured dog and somewhat lighter for the brown or orange particoloured. Ears of medium length, hanging flat. Neck short, round and without throatiness. Body not too short with rather broad, not too deep chest and well-rounded ribs. Legs moderately long and strongly boned. Feet round. Tail long. Coat long and lank, well-feathered, short on the head.

Character affectionate, intelligent, obedient, calm, good watch-dog.

287 Vizsla, Rövidszörü Magyar (Short-haired Hungarian Vizsla)

Origin and use this breed originated in Hungary from the crossing of indigenous hounds, the yellow Birddog imported from Turkey, German trackers and several gundogs. It took more than fifty years before all the desired qualities bred pure. The result is a beautiful and very versatile gundog, which attracts considerable interest in many countries.

Appearance Head lean, broad and moderately long skull, equally long, strong, blunt-ending muzzle, moderately deep stop. Eyes a shade darker than the coat, with intelligent, attentive expression. Ears rather large, broad and pendulous. Neck of medium length and without throatiness. Body rather short, deep, moderately broad chest and moderately arched ribs. Legs long and strongly boned. Feet round. Tail docked to two thirds. Coat short, straight, coarse and glossy.

Character good-tempered, friendly, willing to learn, obedient.

288 Vizsla, Drótszörü Magyar (Rough-haired Hungarian Vizsla)

Origin and use this variety was obtained in the thirties by crossing the Vizsla with the Deutscher Drahthaariger Vorstehund. The rough coat offers more protection for the heavy work in winter, which requires the dog to retrieve ducks from ice-cold water and sit for hours in a boat.

Appearance similar to that of the short-haired Vizsla but for the coat which is 1–1½ inches (2½–3½ cm) long, consisting of dense, rough hair lying close to the body, with soft undercoat; shorter on head, ears and legs; eyebrows and beard are desirable.

289 Vorstehhund, Drahthaariger Deutscher

Origin and use the rough coat for hunting dogs must have originated long ago from crossing hounds with rough-coated sheep-herding dogs. This is a versatile working dog, especially good for hunting water game.

Appearance Head rather long with broad skull and muzzle. Eyes bright. Ears medium, lying flat. Neck of medium length. Body long with moderately broad, deep chest and well-sprung ribs. Legs moderately long and strongly boned. Feet round. Tail docked. Coat of medium length, very hard, lying flat; there are noticeable eyebrows and a not too long beard.

Character intelligent, obedient, lively, keen.

286
Height at withers:
dog: 20 inches
(51 cm), bitch:
somewhat less.
Colour: black and
white, blue and white,
brown and white,
orange and white.

287
Height at withers:
dog: $22\frac{1}{2}$–$25\frac{1}{2}$ inches
($57\frac{1}{2}$–64 cm), bitch:
somewhat less.
Colour: dark wheaten.

289
Height at withers:
dog: 24–26 inches
(61–66 cm), bitch:
not less than $22\frac{1}{2}$
inches (57 cm).
Colour:
inconspicuous;
mostly solid liver roan
or pepper and salt.

290 Vorstehhund, Kurzhaariger Deutscher (Short-haired German Pointer)

Origin and use in the nineteenth century the heavy old German gundog who still carried the blood of the hounds and trackers and of the Spanish Pointer, was repeatedly crossed with Spanish Pointers in order to make it swifter and more high spirited. Now the breed is one of the most widespread and most used gundogs. In contrast to the English gundogs, who are most specialized in the various aspects of hunting, the German Vorstehhund is very versatile.

Appearance Head lean and well-chiselled, sufficiently broad skull, long, strong muzzle, distinct stop. **Eyes** middle-sized and brown. **Ears** moderately long, hanging flat. **Neck** fairly long, as little throatiness as possible. **Body** long with deep moderately broad chest and well-sprung ribs. **Legs** fairly long and strongly boned. **Tail** docked. **Coat** short, dense, coarse and hard.
Character energetic, friendly, obedient, faithful.

291 Vorstehhund, Langhaariger Deutscher

Origin and use this dog is said to originate from crossing the Wachtelhund or Bird dog, already known in the Middle Ages and the French Épagneuls. Some people believe that at a later date the Gordon Setter has also been used. The Langhaar carries less Pointer blood than the Kurzhaar. It is an excellent, versatile gundog.

Appearance Head long cast and lean, the rather broad skull and muzzle are equally long. **Eyes** as dark as possible. **Ears** rather broad and long, hanging flat. **Neck** moderately long and strong. **Body** short, with deep, not too broad chest and arched ribs. **Legs** moderately long and strongly boned. **Feet** moderately long and round. **Tail** long. **Coat** long, 1–2 inches (2½–5 cm) on back and sides, slightly longer on breast and belly, good feathering, hair on head short.
Character intelligent, obedient, lively, faithful.

292 Weimaraner

Origin and use about the end of the eighteenth century this type of dog was more purely bred at the Court of Weimar, hence its name. Carries little or no pointer blood and is less swift than the other German gundogs.
Appearance Head rather narrow, long skull and long, not pointed muzzle, very little stop. **Eyes** amber. **Ears** supple, fairly long, not hanging too flat. **Neck** of medium length, without throatiness. **Body** rather long with deep, not too broad chest and slightly arched ribs. **Legs** rather long and strongly boned. **Feet** short and strong. **Tail** docked. **Coat** for short-haired short, fine and hard; for rough-haired dense, hard and wiry; for long-haired 1–2 inches (2½–5 cm) long, somewhat longer on neck, breast and belly, well-feathered.
Character friendly, obedient, courageous.

290

Height at withers:
dog: 25–26 inches
(63½–66 cm), bitch:
somewhat smaller.
Colour: solid liver;
liver with slight white
or speckled markings
on breast and legs;
dark liver roan with
liver head and larger or
smaller liver patches;
light liver roan with
liver head with or
without larger or
smaller liver patches;
white with liver. All
combinations
mentioned with
black instead of liver.

291

Height at withers:
usually somewhat
smaller than the
Kurzhaar, about 24–25
inches (61–63½ cm).
Colour: solid liver or
liver with white.

292

Height at withers:
dog: 23–25 inches
(58½–63½ cm), bitch:
22–24 inches
(56–61 cm).
Colour: silver-fawn
or mouse-grey. Head
and ears usually
somewhat lighter.
Slight white
markings on breast
and legs allowed.

293 Wetterhound

Origin and use sportsmen from the province of Friesland in the Netherlands used this ancient breed for hunting water game, and especially the otter, which abounded there in former times. The Wetterhound is courageous and keen enough to attack the otter. These two qualities preserved the breed from extinction. After the Wetterhound had been ousted from hunting water game by foreign breeds, it remained a popular watch-dog and polecat and mole catcher.

Appearance Head robust, broad skull, broad, blunt muzzle as long as the skull, slight stop. **Eyes** dark brown for the black and blue roan, brown for the brown dogs. **Ears** of medium length, hanging flat. **Neck** short, strong and round. **Body** with short, broad, deep chest and rounded ribs. **Legs** moderately long and strongly boned. **Feet** round. **Tail** curled. **Coat** dense, tight, curls all over except on the head; the tail ending in a plume.

Character courageous, vicious, independent, good watch-dog.

294 Braque de Bourbonnais

Origin and use the breed was fixed about the turn of the century in the Bourbonnais, central France, where it had been best preserved. Although these gundogs are good working dogs, the breed has never attained any fame outside its native country and it is threatened with extinction.

Appearance Head long, moderately broad skull, long, broad muzzle and slight stop. **Eyes** dark amber. **Ears** long, hanging in slight folds. **Neck** short, with slight throatiness. **Body** with deep broad chest and arched ribs. **Legs** rather long and strongly boned. **Tail** docked to 1–2 inches (2½–5 cm). **Coat** dense, short and oily. **Height at withers** 20–30 inches (51–58½ cm). **Colour** white speckled with light chestnut brown, chestnut patches on head, yellow patches above the eyes, on lips and feet.

295 Braque Dupuy

Origin and use this French gundog originated from a cross between a greyhound and the Braque Français and bears the name of its breeders, the brothers Dupuy. The breed is now very rare. It was used for hunting in water as well as on land.

Appearance the very large, elegant appearance of this gundog clearly betrays his greyhound forebears. **Head** long and narrow, without stop. **Eyes** golden or brown, with gentle, sad expression. **Ears** rather long, thin, hanging in folds. **Neck** long. **Body** with deep, narrow chest and flat ribs. **Legs** long and strongly boned. **Feet** long. **Tail** long. **Coat** more or less short, hard, smooth, finer on head and ears. **Height at withers** dog: about 27 inches (68½ cm); bitch: about 26 inches (66 cm). **Colour** white with small or large chestnut patches or mantle, with or without specks in the white.

293
Height at withers:
dog: 22 inches
(56 cm).
Colour: black, brown
or blue roan.

296 Cesky Funsek

Origin and use this gundog from Czechoslovakia is closely related to
the Stichelhaariger Deutscher Vorstehhund and also carries the blood of the
Drahthaariger Deutscher Vorstehhund and the Griffon.
Appearance this breed is similar to that of the Stichelhaar except for the
coat, which is trifold. It consists of a dense, short undercoat which dis-
appears altogether in summer, a topcoat 2 inches (5 cm) long, which lies
close to the body and 2½ inch (6 cm) long hairs which stick out of the
uppercoat. **Colour** deep dark brown; white sprinkled with brown, white
with brown markings on head and large patches on body.

297 Vorstehhund, Stichelhaariger Deutscher

Origin and use the Stichelhaar, the elder breed of the two rough-haired
varieties, was revived by a Frankfurt breeder in 1865. Nowadays the breed
is less popular than the Drahthaar.
Appearance this dog looks very similar to the Drahthaar except for the
eyes, which are light to dark, brown, and the **coat** which is rough, hard and
stiff, about 1½ inches (4 cm) long, does not lie too close to the body and,
especially in winter, has a good undercoat.
Colour: liver and white; grey and brown mingled, with large or small dark
liver patches.
Height at withers: 24–26 inches (61–66 cm).

Large companion dogs

A very mixed company is assembled in this group, among which are included descendants of mastiffs, terriers, spitz and hunting dogs. The representatives of these breeds have been brought together here not, as was the case with the previous groups, because of their natural disposition for a special kind of work, but because they all make excellent house dogs.

The Pug, the French Bulldog and Boston Terrier will be happy in a quiet household and they will be good company for elderly people taking a stroll, but their owners must be able to accept their snoring for they snore to express their state of mind, as well as in their sleep. The Basenji, is somewhat self-willed, and does not like being led, which makes him totally unsuited to life in crowded surroundings with heavy traffic, where he risks being run over. The same goes for the Chow Chow, also an independent personality, who likes to go pioneering entirely by himself. Both these breeds together with the Kees and the Tibetan Terrier, are a good choice for people living alone, because all four of them attach themselves very much to one single person.

The other breeds are all agreeable family dogs, lively and happy, following the mistress around the house, exuberantly greeting the master and the children at their homecoming and always ready for an escapade with one or all the members of the family. The smaller breeds are more suitable where there are young children, while the large and middle size Poodle and the Dalmatian are ideal, playful companions for teenagers.

The most curious figure in this heterogenous collection is the Mexican Hairless Dog. He is sometimes seen at shows in England and on the Continent, as also is another quite hairless breed, the Chinese Crested Dog, which belongs to the next group. The third type of hairless dog is the Abyssinian or African Sand Terrier, which is rarely or never seen outside his own territory. The various kinds of hairless dogs must undoubtedly be related to each other and it is generally assumed that all of them originate from Africa. The body temperature of these animals is higher than that of normal-coated dogs and their set of teeth is said to be incomplete. A serious study has not yet been made of the causes of their lack of hair, but it is supposed that one or more hormones indispensable for the growth of hair has failed and it could also be a result of mutation. However, the little Mexican will not give the housewife cause for annoyance at moulting time and he is the obvious companion for people allergic to dog-hair.

298 Basenji

Origin and use many dogs similar in type to the breed which is now called Basenji are found throughout central Africa. The forebears of the Basenji came to England from the former Belgian Congo and south Sudan. In their country of origin the dogs are used to destroy rats and other vermin in the neighbourhood of the negro kraals and to track and drive game. As they do this without giving tongue, a wooden bell is hung around their neck. They seldom bark and give a queer whining sound, but they are not dumb as is often asserted.

Appearance Head narrows toward the point of the nose, moderately broad skull, muzzle somewhat shorter than the skull, little stop. **Eyes** dark with inscrutable expression. **Ears** small, thin prick ears. **Neck** long and strong. **Body** short, deep, rather broad chest and well-sprung ribs. **Legs** long and lightly boned. **Feet** small and narrow. **Tail** curled. **Coat** short, smooth and fine.

Character intelligent, affectionate, independent, not very obedient.

299 Bouledogue Français (French Bulldog)

Origin and use nothing is quite certain about the origin of this small Bulldog: the French claim him as a national breed, the English consider him to be a descendant of the Bulldog. The latter came to France in 1850 with lacemakers from Nottingham who crossed to Normandy taking small Bulldogs with them. It is also possible that the Belgian Griffon and Brabançon as well as the Pug have been involved.

Appearance Head square, broad, short skull with skin-folds, broad square muzzle, the lower jaw somewhat longer than the upper jaw, deep stop. **Eyes** dark, somewhat convex, with lively expression. **Ears** bat ears. **Neck** short without throatiness. **Body** short with broad, deep chest, round ribs and arched loins. **Legs** short, hindlegs somewhat longer than forelegs and heavily boned. **Feet** cat-feet. **Tail** short, knobbly or with a hook sideways. **Coat** short, dense, soft and glossy.

Character eager to learn, sensitive, affectionate, calm, not a yapper.

300 Caniche (Poodle)

Origin and use both France and Germany claim the Poodle as a national breed. The French consider him to be descended from the Barbet; the Germans count among his forebears a long-haired shepherding-dog and a gundog or another hunting breed. Anyway it is a very ancient breed, originally used for hunting water-game. 'Caniche', the French name for the breed, is thought to come from 'canard' (duck). The FCI recognized it as a French breed. The Poodle has now spread all over the world and is a very popular house dog, not used for hunting any more. In England the Poodle is bred in more colours than are recognized by the FCI standard.

Appearance Head long cast, moderately broad, long skull, somewhat shorter, strong muzzle, very slight stop. **Eyes** black or dark brown; for brown dogs, dark amber with fiery expression. **Ears** long, lying flat. **Neck** moderately long, strong, without throatiness. **Body** elongated, rather broad, deep chest, arched ribs. **Legs** long with good bones. **Feet** small, oval. **Tail** docked to a third or a half. **Coat** for curly-coated: copious, woolly, curled; for corded Poodle (not occurring any more), long woolly cords.

Character intelligent, obedient, happy, eager to learn.

298

Height at withers:
dog: about 17 inches
(43 cm), bitch: about
16 inches (40½ cm).
Colour: bright tan or
black or black with
tan markings; always
with white feet, breast
and point of tail.

299

Height at withers:
10–14 inches
(26½–35½ cm).
Colour: brindle,
white and brindle,
or fawn.

300

Height at withers:
standard Poodle:
18–22 inches
(45½–56 cm),
miniature Poodle:
14–18 inches
(35½–45½ cm).
According to British
and American
standards standard
Poodle: above 15
inches (38 cm),
miniature Poodle:
11–15 inches
(28–38 cm).
Colour: white, black,
brown, grey. In Britain
any solid colour.

301 Cavalier King Charles Spaniel

Origin and use with the advent in England of the Pekingese, the Japanese Spaniel and the Pug, the broad heads with very flat noses came into fashion and with the help of the Japanese Spaniel, the King Charles was modelled to this type. About 1926 breeders started to re-breed the old type with the longer nose and this new 'old breed' was called the Cavalier King Charles Spaniel.

Appearance Head broad skull of medium length, broad muzzle about $1\frac{1}{2}$ inch (4 cm) long, shallow stop. Eyes large and dark. Ears long, hanging flat. Neck rather short. Body with moderately broad, sufficiently deep chest and well-sprung ribs. Legs not too short and not too heavily boned. Feet oval. Tail long, docked or not. Coat long, silky, smooth or slightly wavy; short on head and well-feathered.

Character lively, sporting, unafraid, happy, good with children.

302 Chow Chow

Origin and use this very ancient breed has been known for many centuries all over China as is evidenced by pictures dating from earliest history. The Chow Chow was used as a house dog, watch-dog and for hunting and even as a source of food. In the north of the country it was also used as a sleigh dog.

Appearance Head with heavy, broad skull, medium long muzzle, broad over its whole length, little stop, blue tongue and gums. Eyes small, black; lighter eyes allowed with blue coat. Ears small prick ears. Neck strong and broad. Body short, with broad, deep chest and well-sprung ribs. Legs of medium length and very heavily boned, the hindlegs perfectly straight without any bend in the stifle and hock. Feet cat-feet. Tail curled. Coat rather long, profuse, dense, straight, with a soft, woolly undercoat.

Character self-assertive, independent, stubborn, aloof, courageous.

303 Chow Chow (Smooth-coated)

Appearance similar to that of the rough-coated except for the **coat** which is short, about $1\frac{1}{2}$ inches (4 cm) long and dense.

304 Dalmatian

Origin and use it is unlikely that they came from Dalmatia, in present-day Yugoslavia, although their name seems to suggest this. Quite unjustly the FCI recognized the breed as Yugoslavian. The breed as it is known nowadays has been developed entirely in England, where crossings took place with the Pointer and later with the Bull Terrier, this latter cross not being a happy one. The breed now occurs in many countries and is no longer used any more. It has always had a great affinity with horses and in times past accompanied its owners, running under the carriage or trap.

Appearance Head rather long, rather broad skull, long, strong muzzle, moderate stop. Eyes dark for black-patched, amber for liver-patched dogs. Ears moderately large and pendulous. Neck rather long, without throatiness. Body with not too broad, deep chest and well-sprung ribs. Legs long with strong, round bones. Feet round. Tail long. Coat short, hard, smooth.

Character happy, attentive, good with children, good watch-dog.

301
Weight: 10–18 lb
(4½–8 kg).
Colour: black with tan
markings; solid red;
chestnut on white
with symmetrical
markings on head;
black and white with
tan markings.

302
Height at withers:
at least 18 inches
(45 cm).
Colour: solid black,
red, fawn, cream,
blue, white.

304
Height at withers:
dog: 23–24 inches
(57½–60 cm), bitch:
22–23 inches
(55–57½ cm).
Colour: white with
round, black or liver
spots.

305 Deutscher Grosspitz (Keeshond)

Origin and use although the Netherlands claimed the Grey Keeshond as a national breed because the Keeshond has long been the watch-dog of the people, especially the bargemen, in that country, the FCI recognize it as German. The Spitz has been known for many centuries in Germany; in Würtemberg mostly black and in Westphalia mostly brown ones were bred. The first Keeshonds to arrive in Holland probably came from Germany as watch-dogs on the barges which plied on the Rhine. From the Netherlands they reached England and the English name for the breed has remained the same as the Dutch. The Keeshond is an excellent watch-dog which does not leave its post.

Appearance Head wedge-shaped, moderately broad skull, rather short, narrowing muzzle, moderate stop. **Eyes** dark. **Ears** small, triangular prick the people, especially the bargemen, in that country, the FCI recognize it **Legs** of medium length and strongly boned. **Feet** small and round. **Tail** curled. **Coat** profuse, long, straight, standing off; woolly undercoat; short and dense on face, ears and front of legs.

Character lively, good watch-dog, one-man dog, distrustful of strangers, yappy.

306 Harlekinpinscher (Harlequin Pinscher)

Origin and use the Harlekinpinscher, recognized in 1958, is the most recent of the German pinscher breeds. He is used in his native country and in Austria as a house and watch-dog and to catch rats and mice.

Appearance Head moderately broad and long skull, broad muzzle of medium length and little stop. **Eyes** preferably dark. **Ears** small prick ears or docked. **Neck** without throatiness. **Body** short, deep chest and moderately arched ribs. **Legs** long and well-boned. **Feet** small and round. **Tail** usually docked short. **Coat** short and glossy.

Character lively, bold, attentive.

307 Islandsk Hund

Origin and use this breed which has existed for many centuries in Iceland, and rarely found in England, had a standard established for it in Denmark in 1898. The breed was recognized by the British Kennel Club, but it is now scarce in its own country. The Islandsk Hund is a watch-dog and is also often used for driving horses and sheep. It lacks the hunting instinct characteristic of most other nordic breeds.

Appearance Head with broad skull, rather short muzzle ending in a point. **Eyes** dark. **Ears** broad, triangular prick ears. **Neck** rather short. **Body** rather short, broad, deep chest. **Legs** moderately long and rather lightly boned. **Feet** long. **Tail** curled. **Coat** of medium length, dense, lying close to the body, short on head and legs.

Character lively, faithful, good watch-dog.

305

Height at withers: for wolf-greys: at least 18 inches (45 cm), for the other colours: at least 16 inches (40 cm).
Colour: for wolf-grey: silver-grey with black hair points. For the other colours: black, white, brown.

306

Height at withers: 12—14 inches (30—35 cm).
Colour: patched on white or light ground; grey with large black or dark patches; brindle with or without tan.

307

Height at withers: 12—16 inches (30—40 cm).
Colour: brownish, greyish, drab white, yellowish. These colours often with drab white neck, collar, face, legs, underside of the body and tail.

308 Kromfohrländer

Origin and use after the Second World War a litter was born at the estate of Kromfohrland in Nassau-Siegen, Germany, out of a Rough-haired Fox Terrier bitch and a Griffon Fauve de Bretagne sire. The owner was so delighted with this litter that she decided to try and obtain a breed which would continue the outward appearance of these dogs. After ten years of breeding she attained her object in so far as the FCI recognized the breed.
Appearance Head wedge-shaped, moderately broad skull, blunt muzzle, slight stop. **Eyes** dark. **Ears** triangular and pendulous. **Neck** of medium length. **Body** elongated, deep, not too broad chest and slightly arched ribs. **Legs** rather long. **Feet** short and round. **Tail** long. **Coat** short, straight and rough; slight beard.
Character intelligent, faithful, good watch-dog.

309 Xoloitzcuintli (Mexican Hairless Dog)

Origin and use the Hairless Dogs were first imported between 1580 and 1600 to Mexico from the Far East with which there was much sea traffic. The breed was maintained in the province of Guerrero, around the port of Acapulco. The dogs were revered in a cult connected with the God Xoloth, whose name is to be found in that of the breed.
Appearance Head rather narrow skull, fairly long, pointed muzzle, slight stop. **Eyes** hazel or dark. **Ears** prick ears. **Neck** rather long. **Body** with broad, fairly deep chest and well-sprung ribs. **Legs** rather long and not too heavily boned. **Feet** hare-feet. **Tail** long. **Coat** hairless, with sometimes a crest of hair on the skull and on the point of the tail.
Character lively, intelligent, affectionate, obedient.

310 Pug

Origin one of the oldest toy breeds which most probably has its origin in China. Dutch sailors took the dogs to their country, from where they spread and came to England in the period of William and Mary. Hence, the misleading appellation of Dutch Pugs.
Appearance Head a loose skin, with large and deep wrinkles. It is massive and round with extremely short, square muzzle; the nose touches the skull. **Eyes** dark, very large, globular in shape, with a questioning expression. **Ears** small, thin, either rose or button ears; preference should be given to the latter. **Neck** thick with dewlaps. **Body** short, cobby and wide in the chest. **Legs** of moderate length and strong. **Feet** between cat- and hare-feet, with black nails. **Tail** curled tightly over the hip. **Coat** short, soft and shiny.
Character funny, headstrong, touchy, brave.

308
Height at withers:
15–18½ inches
(38–46 cm).
Colour: white with
brown on ears, around
the eyes, on skull and
back. Saddle parted in
two by a white stripe
is preferable.
Root of tail should
be brown.

309
Height at withers:
about 16–20 inches
(40–50 cm).
Colour of the skin:
any colour, also
patched; usually
elephant grey or pink.

310
Weight: 14–18 lb
(6·3–8 kg).
Colour: silver, apricot,
fawn, or black; the
light colours with
black mask, black ears
and trace.

311 Shiba Inu

Origin and use the Shiba Inu is the smallest of the three original Japanese breeds. Although it is unquestionably an ancient breed which originated in central Japan, it was not recognized until 1928. It does not often occur outside its own country. The Shiba Inu is a good little watch-dog and vermin catcher.

Appearance Head rather short and broad skull, rather short muzzle ending in a point, slight stop. **Eyes** dark brown. **Ears** small, triangular prick ears. **Neck** of medium length. **Body** not too short with broad, deep chest and well-sprung ribs. **Legs** moderately long and well-boned. **Feet** short. **Tail** curled. **Coat** not too long, hard, dense, standing off the body; with a dense, woolly undercoat.

Characteristic lively, friendly, good watch-dog.

312 Terrier, Boston

Origin and use this American breed originated in the second half of the nineteenth century in and around Boston, Massachusetts, from crossings of the English Bulldog, the coloured Bull Terrier and the French Bulldog. In its own country and in England it is a popular show and house dog which also occurs, though less frequently, in other countries.

Appearance Head square skull, short, square muzzle, distinct stop. **Eyes** dark with friendly and intelligent expression. **Ears** prick ears; in the United States they are docked. **Neck** of medium length. **Body** short, deep, broad chest and well-sprung ribs. **Legs** long and well boned. **Feet** small and round. **Tail** short, straight or screw-shaped. **Coat** short and glossy.

Character lively, intelligent, obedient.

313 Terrier, Tibetan

Origin and use this breed is used by the nomadic tribes in Tibet for herding cattle in mountain country too difficult for larger dogs. The breed is presumed to be related to the Hungarian Puli. The name it bears is misleading in so far it has nothing to do with Terriers. Outside his native country, the Tibetan Terrier is a well-liked house and watch-dog.

Appearance Head not too broad skull of medium length, somewhat shorter, not too broad muzzle, slight stop. **Eyes** dark. **Ears** not too large, hanging not too close to the head. **Neck** of medium length. **Body** square and well-sprung ribs. **Legs** moderately long and well-boned. **Feet** large and round. **Tail** curled. **Coat** long, fine, smooth or wavy, not silky or woolly; with a fine and woolly undercoat.

Character lively, intelligent, courageous, not pugnacious, good watch-dog, one-man dog.

311

Height at withers:
dog: 15–16 inches
(37½–40 cm), bitch:
14–15 inches
(35–37½ cm).
Colour: red, pepper
and salt, red-grey,
black-grey, black,
black and tan,
patched, white.

312

Weight: light weight:
under 15 lb (7 kg),
middle weight:
15–19 lb (7–8½ kg),
heavy weight:
19–25 lb (8½–11 kg).
Colour: brindle with
symmetrical white
markings; black
instead of brindle
allowed.

313

Height at withers:
14–16 inches
(35–40 cm).
Colour: white, golden,
cream, grey, smoky,
black, bicoloured or
tricoloured.

Small companion dogs

The dogs belonging to this final group, like those of the preceding group, were not selected according to their qualities of character, but because of their small size. As a result, this group, like that of the large companion dogs, is a very heterogeneous one. Lovers of terriers, spaniels, spitz, poodles and greyhounds who for some reason are not able to keep larger dogs, will find in this group their favourite breeds in miniature size.

For terrier admirers there are the Australian, Black and Tan and Yorkshire Terriers together with the terriers of Germany: the Affenpinscher and the Zwergpinscher and the Miniature Schnauzer. All of them have the correct terrier character: they are lively and keen.

The spaniel enthusiasts have a large choice of the very short-muzzled Pekingese, the Japanese, and the King Charles Spaniels. If, however, they prefer the peculiar shape of the face with the nose very close to the forehead, they may also like the Belgian Brabançon and Griffons, although, of course, these are not spaniels. Those who prefer a more normal muzzle can choose between the Tibetan Spaniel and the two Papillon varieties.

For those who like spitz and want the dog to be a good watch-dog, the Pomeranian or the Schipperke are ideal. The light, grace-ful Italian Greyhound will undoubtedly appeal to the greyhound's admirers.

The Poodle lovers will find here the Miniature Poodle and the closely related Bichons. They are all said to descend from the small Barbet, the old French long-curled dog for water hunting. Long ago small, long-haired, mostly white dogs appeared in the countries around the Mediterranean, from which, eventually, five breeds developed: the Maltese, the Bolognese, the Havanais, the Bichon à Poil Frisé and the Petit Chien Lion. The collective name for these breeds is said to have originated from the diminutive for Barbet: Barbichon, whence Bichon.

Dog lovers who like a long-coated pet will appreciate the Shih Tzu and the Lhasa Apso. Also long-haired, though only with two tufts, one on the skull and one on the tail-tip, is the elegant Chinese Crested Dog with its beautifully patched skin. This little naked dog is much more attractive than his larger colleague in the previous group.

Of all the breeds of the world, the Chihuahuas, although they tend to vary in size, can be the smallest, which for many people may be a reason to consider them as the most desirable of toy dogs.

These small representatives of dog breeds should be thought of as true dogs, and should be treated as such. They need plenty of exercise and healthy food just as much as their larger relatives. It is particularly harmful for these small creatures to be crammed with sweets and it is of prime importance that their happiness should never be sacrificed to the maintenance of their beautiful appearance. They should never be prevented from running and romping in order to spare their spotless white or profuse coat. A life of being coddled or shown off is unworthy of any dog.

Scale of Small Companion Dog illustrations 1 :10

314 Affenpinscher

Origin the breed is undoubtedly related to the Belgian Griffons, which perhaps descend from it. Similar dogs already appear in the fifteenth and sixteenth century in paintings by Jan van Eyck and Albrecht Dürer. In the Belgian breeds, the muzzle was totally bred out, so that the nose lies almost flat against the head, but it was kept normal in the Affenpinscher.
Appearance Head rather broad skull, short, not very pointed muzzle, distinct stop. **Eyes** black and sparkling. **Ears** cropped if not congenitally pricked. **Neck** short. **Body** square and lightly boned. **Feet** oval. **Tail** docked. **Coat** hard, fairly long, especially on the head and legs.
Character fiery, quick-tempered, very affectionate, unfriendly to strangers.

315 Bichon à Poil Frisé

Origin the breed probably originated through crossing the Maltese and a small size Barbet, and it is akin to the Miniature Poodle. In the nineteenth century many small white dogs occurred on Tenerife, but the Spanish Kennel Club proved that this breed, in spite of the fact that the name Tenerife had been given to these dogs, was not Spanish. Accordingly, the FCI recognized the breed as Franco-Belgian under the name it now bears.
Appearance Head broad skull, muzzle shorter than the skull, slight stop. **Eyes** dark. **Ears** not too large and pendulous. **Neck** fairly long. **Body** deep, fairly broad chest and rather round ribs. **Legs** rather short with fine bones. **Feet** strong. **Tail** curled. **Coat** 3–5 inches ($7\frac{1}{2}$–$12\frac{1}{2}$ cm) long, fine, woolly, curled; sometimes lion-clipped.
Character lively, happy, affectionate.

316 Bolognese

Origin it is reasonably certain that the breed reached England from the Canary Islands, but it seems to have existed in Bologna in northern Italy, as early as the fifteenth century. Accordingly it was recognized as Italian under the name Bolognese. It seldom occurs outside Italy.
Appearance Head not too long, with broad skull, short, strong muzzle and distinct stop. **Eyes** dark. **Ears** drop ears. **Body** not too short, with broad, deep chest and well-sprung ribs. **Legs** short. **Feet** round. **Tail** curled. **Coat** long, dense, curly, standing off, soft, shorter on the muzzle.
Character slow, calm, reserved.

314

Height at withers: maximum 10 inches (25 cm).
Colour: black, black with light tan, yellow, reddish yellow, red, grey.

315

Height at withers: 11–12 inches (27–30 cm).
Colour: white.

316

Height at withers: maximum 12 inches (30 cm).
Colour: white, some small light yellow patches allowed.

237

317 Caniche Nain (Toy Poodle)

Origin These little dogs were already popular pets at the Court of the French King Louis XVI. Both they and the two larger varieties are descended from the older Barbet breeds. The breed is one of the most widely spread and is very popular in England, the United States and many European countries.

Appearance similar to that of the Caniche, except for the **height at withers** maximum 11 inches (27½ cm).

318 Chihuahua (Long-haired, Short-haired)

Origin the breed bears the name of the Mexican province where it often occurred. It is presumed that it originally lived in the wild and was caught and tamed by the Indians. It is also possible that it is a pygmy breed of a lost civilization, which ran wild and survived in the woods. Its hunting instinct is remarkable for such a very small breed.

Appearance **Head** round, with broad, rounded skull, short, pointed muzzle, deep stop. **Eyes** black, brown, blue or red; light colour allowed for pale-coloured dogs. **Ears** large, prick ears. **Neck** of medium length. round. **Body** elongated, deep chest and well-sprung ribs. **Legs** of moderate length with good bones. **Feet** small. **Tail** long. **Coat** short, dense, glossy and may be short and wavy, with feathering but short ol the head.

Character intelligent, inquisitive, affectionate, courageous.

319 Chinese Crested Dog

Origin they are now extinct in China, where they were once mandarins' pets, but they were purebred there for at least a hundred years.

Appearance **Head** with moderately broad skull, medium long muzzle ending in a point, slight stop. **Eyes** dark. **Ears** pricked. **Neck** rather long. **Body** medium broad, deep chest and well-sprung ribs. **Legs** long and lightly boned. **Feet** oval. **Tail** long. No **coat**, except crest on the head and rather long hair on feet and tip of tail.

Character lively, affectionate, friendly.

317

Height at withers:
maximum 14 inches
(35 cm).
Colour: black, white,
brown, grey.

318

Weight: 2–7½ lb
(0·9–3½ kg).
Colour: all colours
and shades allowed.

319

Weight: 6–12 lb
(2½–5½ kg).
Colour: blue, pink,
golden, mauve; solid
or patched. Darker in
summer than in winter.

320 Deutscher Kleinspitz (Pomeranian)

Origin the Deutscher Kleinspitz were taken to England from Pomerania in Germany, and acquired the name Pomeranian. The first Kleinspitz were rather heavy dogs, but in England they soon were bred smaller and lighter with enormous coats. The white varieties, which are now scarce, were the first to achieve much success in England.

Appearance the same standard is valid for the Deutscher Kleinspitz as for the large German Spitz, but in England, where the Pomeranian is bred much more intensively than in Germany, a standard was established which differs from that of the country of origin. As breeding takes place almost everywhere according to the English type, the characteristics of the English standard are given here. **Head** fox-like, with rather broad skull, short, pointed muzzle, moderate stop. **Eyes** dark with intelligent expression. **Ears** small prick ears. **Neck** rather short. **Body** short with broad, rather deep chest and well-rounded ribs. **Legs** medium length with fine bones. **Feet** small. **Tail** curled over the back. **Coat** long, straight, hard, standing off, woolly, soft undercoat; short and soft on head, front of legs and feet and with much feathering.

Character happy, active, affectionate.

321 Épagneul Nain Continental (Papillon)

Origin similar little dogs occur in countless old pictures, and they have spread all over Europe. The FCI recognized the breed as Franco-Belgian. The prick eared is the most popular of the two existing varieties. It originated by mutation or from crossing with the Zwergspitz. Because of its prick ears it is called Papillon (butterfly).

Appearance **Head** rather short, moderately broad skull, pointed muzzle shorter than the skull, distinct stop. **Eyes** dark. **Ears** prick ears. **Neck** of medium length. **Body** with broad, rather deep chest and well-sprung ribs. **Legs** moderately long with rather fine bones. **Feet** hare-feet. **Tail** long. **Coat** profuse, glossy, wavy, not soft, short on the head, the front of the legs and below the hocks with long feathering.

Character proud, affectionate, friendly.

322 Épagneul Nain Continental (Phalène)

Origin the Phalène must be the oldest of the two varieties of the Épagneul Nain Continental.

Appearance similar to that of the Papillon, except for the **ears** which are pendulous.

323 Griffon Belge

Origin this breed probably originated in the second half of the nineteenth century from crossings of small, long-haired non-descript little dogs with the Affenpinscher and later with the Pug. It is as well known in England and the United States as in Europe.

Appearance **Head** with broad, round skull, very short muzzle, deep stop. **Eyes** protuberant, black. **Ears** prick or crop ears. **Neck** rather short. **Body** with fairly broad, deep chest. **Legs** of medium length. **Feet** round. **Tail** docked to one third. **Coat** half long, hard and shaggy.

Character intelligent, lively, affectionate.

320

Height at withers: maximum 11 inches (28 cm).
Colour: white, black, brown from light to dark; wolf-grey; orange.

321

Height at withers: seldom more than 11 inches (28 cm).
Colour: all colours allowed.

323

Weight: dog: maximum 10 lb ($4\frac{1}{2}$ kg), bitch: 11 lb (5 kg).
Colour: black, black with tan markings, black mingled with brown.

324 Griffon Bruxellois

Origin derived from the Griffon Belge, this variety was named after the Belgian capital.

Appearance similar to that of the Griffon Belge except in **colour** which should be reddish with some black on the moustache and chin allowed, and ears which are semi-erect.

325 Havanais (Havanese)

Origin the forebears of the Havanais probably came to Cuba at the time of the Spanish domination and from there returned to Europe.

Appearance Head with broad skull, pointed muzzle, deep stop. **Eyes** dark. **Ears** hanging with a fold. **Body** not too short and well-sprung ribs. **Legs** moderately short. **Feet** oval. **Tail** curled. **Coat** long, soft and slightly curled at the tips.

Character lively, affectionate.

326 Lhasa Apso

Origin it is assumed that the breed originated through crossing the Tibetan Terrier and the Tibetan Spaniel. The Apso is well represented in the United States and occurs more and more frequently in Europe.

Appearance Head with medium narrow skull, blunt muzzle, the length of which is half that of the skull, slight stop. **Eyes** dark brown. **Ears** pendulous. **Body** elongated with sufficiently deep chest and well-sprung ribs. **Legs** short. **Feet** cat-feet. **Tail** curled. **Coat** long, straight, hard and dense.

Character happy, self-assertive, intelligent, faithful, not friendly to everybody.

324
Weight: dog:
maximum 10 lb
(4½ kg), bitch:
11 lb (5 kg).
Colour: red with
dark mask.

325
Height at withers:
11–13 inches
(28–32 cm).
Colour: white, beige,
chestnut. Large
patches on ears or
body in beige, grey or
black allowed.

326
Height at withers:
dog: 10–11 inches
(25–28 cm), bitch:
somewhat smaller.
Colour: solid; golden,
sandy, honey, dark
grey, slate, reddish;
bicoloured; white with
black or brown.

327 Maltese

Origin this is the oldest of the breeds belonging to the Bichon group from which the other four probably descended. The breed has been named after the island of Malta where it originated. In the fourth century BC Aristotle called these small white dogs ladies' pets and in the Middle Ages they once more came into fashion. Nowadays they may be seen at shows in many European countries and the United States where they may be counted among the really popular breeds.

Appearance Head with flat skull, rather short muzzle, distinct stop. **Eyes** dark, with intelligent expression. **Ears** triangular and pendulous. **Neck** long without throatiness. **Body** not too short and strongly boned. **Feet** round. **Tail** curled. **Coat** very long, average length 9 inches (22 cm), dense, silky and lustrous.

Character intelligent, lively, affectionate.

328 Pekingese

Origin these very ancient Chinese breed are named after the capital of China, where they were court dogs as long ago as the Tang Dynasty of the eighth century. Their theft was punished by execution, nevertheless the first representatives of the breed which reached England in 1860 were stolen from the Summer Palace.

Appearance Head massive, with broad skull, very short, broad, wrinkled muzzle, deep stop. **Eyes** protuberant and dark. **Ears** heart shaped and pendulous. **Body** short with broad chest, round ribs and narrow waist. **Legs** short, crooked and heavily boned, hindlegs lighter, not crooked. **Feet** broad, forefeet turning out slightly. **Tail** long. **Coat** long, straight, hard, thick undercoat and profuse feathering.

Character intelligent, dignified, courageous, lively, self-willed.

329 Petit Brabançon

Origin this breed has the same origin as the Griffons, the short hair came into the breed by crossing with the Pug. At first, these smooth-haired dogs were not wanted, later they were kept and called after the Belgian province of Brabant.

Appearance similar to that of the Griffon Belge except for the **coat,** which is short and the **colour,** which may be reddish, with or without a black mask, or black with tan markings.

327

Height at withers:
dog: 8½–10 inches
(21–25 cm), bitch:
8–9 inches
(20–23 cm).
Colour: white.

328

Weight: dog: 7–11 lb
(3–5 kg), bitch:
8–12 lb (3½–5½ kg).
Colour: all colours and
markings allowed
except for albino and
liver.

329

Weight: dog:
maximum 10 lb
(4½ kg), bitch:
11 lb (5 kg).
Colour: red or
red with a
black mask.

330 Petit Chien Lion

Origin a dog of Mediterranean origin like the Bichons. The type was established by the end of the sixteenth century. Similar little dogs were extensively bred in Belgium. The Bichon à Poil Frisé was recognized by the FCI as a Franco-Belgian breed and curiously enough the Petit Chien Lion as a French one.

Appearance Head short, rather broad skull, pointed muzzle of medium length, distinct stop. **Eyes** dark with intelligent expression. **Ears** pendulous. **Neck** rather long. **Body** short, sufficiently deep chest and well-sprung ribs. **Legs** long with fine bones. **Feet** round. **Tail** long. **Coat** rather long, wavy, lion-clipped.

Character intelligent, lively, affectionate.

331 Piccolo Levriero Italiano

Origin although the breed is called Italian, it certainly did not originate in Italy. It was already known in much earlier times in Egypt and Greece: Cleopatra owned small greyhounds. Much later, it is assumed, King Charles I brought similar little dogs from France to England, and Frederik the Great owned large numbers of them at Potsdam and always took his favourites with him on his campaigns. Many painters have included them in portraits of important persons. Originally the breed was larger and less fine than it is nowadays and these dogs used to catch rabbits, rats and mice. In its present form, smaller and finer, the Piccolo Levriero Italiano was bred in England.

Appearance Head with flat skull, pointed muzzle which is as long as the skull, not very distinct stop. **Ears** rose ears. **Neck** long. **Body** short with arched loins, deep chest and tucked up belly. **Legs** long with fine bones. **Feet** hare-feet. **Tail** long. **Coat** short, smooth and glossy.

Character fiery, intelligent, happy, affectionate, good watch-dog.

332 Schipperke

Origin this breed originated in Flanders, where they competed in rat catching matches. Opinions differ as to whether the breed originated from a crossing of kees and terrier or descends from the sheep-herding dog. The name was first Scheperke, which means shepherd, and gradually changed to Schipperke, meaning 'little skipper', although these little dogs were not used on boats.

Appearance Head foxy, rather broad skull, not too long, sharp muzzle, slight stop. **Eyes** dark brown. **Ears** prick ears. **Neck** strong. **Body** with short, broad, deep chest and well-sprung ribs. **Legs** fairly long and lightly boned. **Feet** round. **Tail** missing. **Coat** rather short, hard, standing off, longer around the neck and at the back of the hindlegs and short on the head.

Character faithful, lively, noisy, good watch-dog, unfriendly to strangers, good ratter.

330

Height at withers:
8–14 inches
(20–35 cm).
Colour: all colours
allowed, solid as well
as bicoloured. Colours
most wanted: white,
black, lemon.

331

Height at withers:
dog: 13–14 inches
(33–35 cm), bitch:
12½–14 inches
(32–35 cm).
Colour: solid black,
slate-grey, isabella,
white on chest and
toes allowed.

332

Weight: large size:
11–20 lb (5–9 kg),
small size: 6½–11 lb
(3–5 kg).
Colour: solid black.

333 Shih Tzu

Origin there are two opinions about the origin of this breed. It originated in China from crossing either the Pekingese and the Tibetan Terrier, or the Lhasa Apso and the Pekingese. The Shih Tzu has been known in England since 1930 and is seen regularly at shows there and in other countries. In the United States the breed was not known until 1960.

Appearance **Head** broad and round with short, square muzzle, distinct stop. **Eyes** dark. **Ears** large and pendulous. **Body** elongated with broad, deep chest and well-sprung ribs. **Legs** short with good bones. **Feet** strong. **Tail** curled. **Coat** long, dense, straight with a dense undercoat.

Character intelligent, lively, independent.

334 Spaniel, Japanese

Origin these small dogs, which were the forebears• of the present Pekingese, were taken to Japan by Buddhist priests. About the year 800 they were very popular with the Japanese nobility. Today, the breed is represented at most shows in Europe and the United States.

Appearance **Head** large with broad skull, rounded in front, very short, broad muzzle, deep stop. **Eyes** dark. **Ears** small and pendulous. **Neck** rather short. **Body** short with broad, deep chest. **Legs** rather short with fine bones. **Feet** small hare-feet. **Tail** curled. **Coat** long, straight, soft and silky; short on the head; good feathering.

Character happy, intelligent, lively.

335 Spaniel, King Charles

Origin in the seventeenth century Sir Anthony van Dyck painted King Charles I with his dogs, and his fondness for the breed caused it to be called after him. At the beginning of our century an attempt was made to re-name it the English Toy Spaniel, but King Edward VII, who was a great lover of the breed, protested and the name King Charles Spaniel was retained. The four types of colouring in which the breed occurs all bear a separate name. These spaniels are seldom seen outside Britain.

Appearance **Head** with arched, broad skull, square, very short, upturned muzzle, very distinct stop. **Eyes** large and dark. **Ears** long, hanging flat. **Body** with broad, deep chest, and well-sprung ribs. **Legs** short with good bones. **Feet** rather large. **Tail** usually docked half way. **Coat** long, silky, straight, slight wave allowed and profuse feathering.

Character affectionate, attentive, good watch-dog.

333

Height at withers: maximum 10½ inches (27 cm).
Colour: all colours. White blaze on forehead and white point at tail are much appreciated.

334

Height at withers: dog: about 12 inches (30 cm), bitch: somewhat smaller.
Colour white with black, white with red in several shades.

335

Weight: 8–14 lb (3½–6 kg).
Colour: King Charles: black and tan; Prince Charles: white and black with tan markings; Ruby: chestnut; Blenheim: white with chestnut.

336 Spaniel, Tibetan

Origin this spaniel was bred mostly in the border valleys between Tibet and China, where it was a beloved pet of women and priests.
Appearance Head medium sized with moderately broad skull, short, blunt muzzle, slight stop. Eyes brown. Ears pendulous. Body elongated with medium broad chest. Legs short, slightly crooked forelegs. Feet hare-feet. Tail curled. Coat rather long, smooth flat; woolly undercoat and good feathering; it is short on head and front of the legs.
Character independent, lively, self-assertive, not friendly to everybody.

337 Terrier, Australian Silky

Origin this Australian breed was first called Sydney Silky Terrier. It originated from crossing the Yorkshire Terrier and the Australian Terrier.
Appearance Head wedge-shaped, skull not too broad and slightly longer than the muzzle, not too deep stop. Eyes dark with an intelligent expression. Ears prick ears. Neck thin and moderately long. Body long with moderately broad, rather deep chest. Legs short and lightly boned. Feet cat feet. Tail docked. Coat 5—6 inches (13—15 cm) long, flat, silky, glossy, short on pasterns and feet.
Character intelligent, lively, happy.

338 Terrier, English Toy (Black and Tan Terrier, Toy Manchester Terrier)

Origin the old rough-haired Black and Tan Terrier, forebear of many English terrier breeds, was also the ancestor of the Manchester Terrier, out of which, with the help of Whippets and Italian Greyhound, the English Toy Terrier was derived. These little dogs are excellent rat catchers.
Appearance Head long with narrow skull, narrowing muzzle, slight stop. Eyes small and dark. Ears prick ears. Neck rather long. Body rather short with narrow, deep chest and well-sprung ribs. Legs long. Feet more cat-than hare-feet. Tail long. Coat short, dense, and glossy.
Character one-man dog, affectionate, distrustful of strangers, good watch-dog.

336

Height at withers:
dog: maximum 11
inches (28 cm), bitch:
maximum 9½ inches
(24 cm).
Colour: golden yellow,
reddish, black, black
and tan, white with
dark patches, cream,
white, brown.

337

Height at withers:
9 inches (22½ cm).
Colour: blue, silver-
dove or slate-blue with
tan on muzzle and
cheeks, around the
ears, on the pasterns
and the underside of
the tail.

338

Height at withers:
10–12 inches
(25–30 cm).
Colour: jet black with
mahogany markings.

339 Terrier, Yorkshire

Origin the breed originated in Leeds and Halifax, in Yorkshire, England in the second half of the nineteenth century. The Skye Terrier and the Manchester Terrier were probably used in its development, and perhaps the Dandie Dinmont Terrier and the Maltese were also introduced. The Yorkshire Terrier attracts increasing public attention in England and elsewhere.

Appearance Head small with flat skull, rather short muzzle, distinct stop. **Eyes** dark with fiery, intelligent expression. **Ears** small prick ears. **Body** short with straight back. **Legs** short and lightly boned. **Feet** as round as possible. **Tail** docked halfway. **Coat** long, straight, glossy and silky.

Character courageous, intelligent, lively, sporting.

340 Zwergpinscher (Miniature Pinscher)

Origin of the many types of Pinschers which have long been known in Germany, the Zwergpinscher followed the Pinscher and the Schnauzer in developing as an independent breed. It is very popular in many European countries and in the United States.

Appearance Head long cast, flat skull, strong muzzle, moderate stop. **Eyes** almost black. **Ears** prick ears, or cropped according to the standard of the country of origin, but in other countries button ears. **Neck** rather long. **Body** short with deep chest and well-sprung ribs. **Legs** of medium length with good bones. **Feet** cat-feet. **Tail** docked to three vertebrae. **Coat** short, dense, smooth, and glossy.

Character bold, intelligent, passionate, attentive.

341 Zwergschnauser (Miniature Schnauzer)

Origin it is believed that the forebears of the Zwergschnauzer may be the smaller specimens of the middle sized Schnauzer, perhaps crossed with the Affenpinscher. The breed is popular both in Europe and the United States.

Appearance Head long with flat skull, strong muzzle, moderate stop. **Eyes** dark. **Ears** prick ears, or cropped according to the standard of Germany, the country of origin; in other countries button ears. **Neck** long without throatiness. **Body** short, with moderately broad, very deep chest and moderately-sprung ribs. **Legs** of medium length with good bones. **Feet** cat-feet. **Tail** docked to three vertebrae. **Coat** rough, hard, with shaggy eyebrows and beard.

Character lively, daredevil, obedient, affectionate, not friendly to everybody.

339
Weight: up to 7 lb
(3 kg).
Colour: dark steel
blue from the back of
the head to the root of
the tail, with bright tan
on chest, face, feet,
and cheeks.

340
Height at withers:
10–14 inches
(25–36 cm).
Colour: black with
tan markings.

341
Height at withers:
12–14 inches
(30–35 cm).
Colour: pepper and
salt; black.

Index

Dog numbers are indicated by the heavier type.